ISLAND WALKS

BOOK ONE

Lindisfarne to Iona

Paul Truswell

First published in the United Kingdom in 2021 by
The Choir Press
ISBN 978-1-78963-248-4

Contents

Acknowledgements

All of my long walks are solo but that in no way means that others are not involved, far from it; in fact without the encouragement of my first love, wife since 1984, and business partner since 2002, I doubt that I would have set foot on any of them. Therefore without a word of hesitation **Janine Truswell**, is top-centre at the head of these notes of thanks; not forgetting her role as 'basecamp manager' for all of my many jaunts into the wild; this being done at the same time as keeping our business going back home and looking after our son **James**, two mad Boradors Max and Meggy, Wabbit and a tank-full of tropical fish. She is a true multi-tasker of formidable capability; definitely a case of 'power behind the throne'.

Whilst in the family department I would also like to thank Janine's niece **Carrie-Anne Pollard** who encouraged me to get on with writing this book and hopefully the others to come. Thanks Carrie, without your nudging and encouragement this budding author would have never got off the starting blocks!

Also, family wise I would like to thank my big bro **David Truswell** and **Janet Truswell** for taking me on my first long walk (when I was barely out of shorts and into long trousers) along the Cornish coast from Porthallow to Lizard Point. That walk in 1971 lit my 'blue touchpaper', and effectively launched my young appetite for long-distance walking. Also, to their friend **Gordon Gange** who I seem to remember gave me my first sight of W.A. Poucher's 'Scottish Peaks' photographic guidebook; another key moment in my developing love for the great outdoors. Thanks again to David and Janet for meeting me at the end of this walk on Iona, such a kind act I will never forget. Thanks also to **Sarah Couperthwaite** my beautiful daughter for lending me her camera just before she got married to **Michael** upon my return from this walk. Mike is an expert dry-stone waller and hedge-layer.

Last but not least in the family department I must acknowledge my late parents **Raymond Truswell** and **Beatrice Mary Truswell** who always encouraged me to see God in Creation, and in particular for taking me as a 10-year-old up Snowdon on the Mountain Railway on a cloudy day in August 1969. That first sight from Clogwyn Station of the Llanberis Pass far below through a break in the clouds was another moment I will never forget; it was as if the whole world was suddenly opening up before me.

Beyond family there are so many, and as always with written acknowledgements there is a danger that I will leave someone out, but I will do my best in the following paragraphs by thanking…

Alfred Wainwright (1907 – 1991) British fellwalker, guidebook author, illustrator, and animal lover; I am proud to be a member of the Wainwright Society in his memory and honour; a man whose love for the English Lake District was manifested with every move of his pen all those years ago. He was and continues to be an inspiration to generations of walkers. Further information at wainwright.org.uk.

The **Scottish Rights of Way and Access Society** (also known as 'Scotways') for all of their route planning advice and their kind letter (reproduced on page 145). Further information: scotways.com

Cre8 Macclesfield and their continuing work to support disadvantaged families in Macclesfield is both revolutionary and life changing. It was my privilege to contribute to their work with the proceeds of this walk. Further information: cre8macclesfield.org and on page six.

All the 'Evergreens' at **Holy Trinity Hurdsfield** parish church in Macclesfield, and especially the minibus gang: **Winnie, Audrey, Evelyn, Maureen, Gill, Lin, Pat, Ruby, Nelly, Sheila, Susan** and the two **Jeans**, who were all prayer warriors on my behalf. Sadly, many of them are no longer with us and have gone to a better place. Further information: hthmacc.com

Miles Bailey of **The Choir Press** who supported me throughout the whole 'getting published' process. His care, attention to detail and willingness to discuss publishing technicalities with patience, and general understanding of me as a new author, is much appreciated and continues to be highly valued.
Further information: selfpublishingbooks.co.uk

Truswell Haulage for free caps! Further information: truswell.co.uk

My best mate **Steve 'Percy' Percival** for inspiration, mad walks, silly driving and making me laugh to heaven and back over the last 40+ years.

Richard Newstead for introducing me to GPS for walkers and the loan of his SatMap Active 10 device.

Last but not least thanks to my close friends **Ricci "Eh Riccarrrrdo!" Downard** for his excellent proof reading, assurances and foreword to this book, and his wife **Karen Downard** for using her sewing skills to repair my gaiters and shirts!

In loving memory of my parents. Always missed, never forgotten.

Raymond Truswell 1922 - 1976

Beatrice Mary Truswell 1922 – 2001 (centre)
Dad on the left, Grandma Doris Chapman on the right
and me with prize-winning knobbly knees at the front.
Picture taken on Stevenage railway station around 1966.

Foreword by Ricci Downard

This book demonstrates why grumpy old geezers should be allowed their grumpiness; and why they should be allowed to wander off on their own sometimes. It does us all a favour. Paulo (for some reason I have always called him Paulo) takes his unpretentious and observant self through a landscape and circumstances he knows and loves well. He follows the fourteen centuries old journey of Saint Aidan across the highlands between Iona and the Tweed, only in the wrong direction. From photos and notes made at the time he recalls his feelings and encounters.

My very good friend Mr. Paul "Eh Paulo!" Truswell is a strange hybrid of extreme extrovert and lone walker. By nature, he is quick to form friendships, opinionated and prickly, principled, with a strong vein of gratitude. On top of these he has two other qualities which make this book really work:

One is his history and qualifications in architecture. He describes cottages, civic infrastructure, and the interior of pubs, properly. Form meets purpose aesthetics and setting. We get the same, mostly appreciative commentary on ways and maps (electronic and paper), ferries, padlocks, and even clothing.

The other is what psychologists might call 'censoriousness'. When Paulo sees a thing, be it fantastic or dreadful, he describes it with accuracy and enthusiasm, immediately. My own walking skills are woeful besides Paulo's, yet he has frequently dragged me out for lengthy assaults on hills in the Peak District, Lake district or even on Skye. Recently I have realised why it is that Paulo sees me as a companion of choice. It is because, being blind, I never have an opinion about his map-reading or which route we should take, or ought to have taken. For my part, as I walk, I am silently devouring his Kodachrome descriptions of everything he sees. In this book, once or twice, Paulo swings the searchlight of his attention inward. His inner workings, history, prayers, briefly shown, are a helpful insight.

Ricci and Karen Downard

Visit Ricci and Karen's website at ricci.org.uk to find out more about them and their campaign:

"In Our Generation We Can Eradicate Extreme Poverty and Unfair Trade"

My friend Ricci 'Ricarrrrdo' Downard enjoying the glories of the Antrim coast in April 2013

Beneficiary • Cre8 Macclesfield

My chosen charitable beneficiary for this walk:

Cre8 Macclesfield Youth & Community Programme comprises a charity and a social enterprise business, all based on the Moss Estate in my home town of Macclesfield. Cre8 is part of the work of St Barnabas Church on Lyme Avenue which is also on the Moss Estate…

Cre8 runs activities and services for children, young people, young adults, and their families, focusing on those who are at risk or hard to reach.

Their social enterprise division, known as Cre8 Facilities, employs young people and young adults doing commercial vehicle washing. Cre8 is a full time programme staffed by qualified youth workers, supported by student youth and community workers, and volunteers, many of whom live on the Moss Estate in Macclesfield.

Further information online at cre8macclesfield.org

Pics used with kind permission granted by Cre8 July 2021

Introduction

Book writing. Who does it? Not me… Until two years ago that is when I made my first tentative keyboard taps with that very ambition in mind, although it has to be said my mind was not totally on the job I had just started. For reasons I cannot fully recall in this book of recollections I was also watching Prime Minister's Questions on BBC Parliament, and in response I was prompted to write the following few lines:

"Great Britain is under threat. Well not all of it, just the 'Great' part. I write this on the 3rd of April 2019 following weeks of deliberations in the House of Commons about implementation of the EU Withdrawal Agreement, at a time of national anxiety and division. Any notion of 'greatness' regarding our standing in the world as a nation, has in recent days been challenged in the media and elsewhere with the world watching."

That was as far as I got; not much further than a wannabe title or at least the inspiration for one. Inexplicably my book writing appetite dissipated like the morning mist. Time elapsed; any idea of a book was on hold. I wrote nothing more until April 2021, hopefully towards the tail-end of a global pandemic.

Even though the above seems like the start of an in-depth politically inspired tome, I hope you are relieved to read that this is not a book about politics. Greatness can indeed become a thing of the past

The author at Land's End in May 2016

or future for any nation, but I was being prompted to write about something far more permanent; the greatness of our island in a geographical sense; our Great Britain.

The following pages are about one of my solo long-distance walks, most recent of which started in Dover but ended prematurely in Edinburgh due to a foot injury, continuing a year later in 2019 to Scourie on Scotland's north-west coast, still falling short of the personal goal that I have not yet reached: Cape Wrath.

God Willing and with co-operation from knees feet and weather, in what I am hoping will be a post-pandemic world, I am planning a third attempt at getting to Cape Wrath from the south coast in 2022 when, all being well, and after two years of postponement, I will head north from the enticingly named Start Point at Devon's south-eastern extremity. When it says "Start" on the map who am I to argue!

On a few occasions I have been asked why I don't just get on and 'do' Land's End to John o' Groats. My response to this is that 'LeJog' as it is sometimes referred to has never really flicked my walking switch. LeJog has been walked, ran, cycled, forwards, backwards, in fancy dress, by wheelchair, skateboard and even stand-up paddleboard (by sea one assumes). All are noble pursuits and deserving of much praise and adulation; but as a route it is not for me, which is odd really because my objectives are not so very different. Naturally most people at some point in their lives desire to be recognised or at least noticed for their achievements. We all, to a greater or lesser degree, want our moment in the spotlight. I am therefore hoping that this book will be appreciated and liked by many and, moreover, I genuinely hope that some might be inspired to take on their own challenge. Distance and means are immaterial really, big numbers look good, but they are not what ultimately matter. Above all, motivation is of prime importance, as is reaching your own personal goal. Not my goal, *your* goal.

Picture used with kind permission granted by The Captain Tom Foundation

The late Captain Sir Thomas Moore, (pictured left) more popularly known as 'Captain Tom' demonstrated this to the nation for all to see. He had a very modest goal, typically English, quietly determined and very well motivated. At the age of ninety-nine he reached his goal and went beyond to the benefit of many. Today he is remembered not so much for the huge sums of money that he raised, but more because of who he was, his personality, his life story, and his determination. Captain Tom inspired a nation at a time of national crisis.
Further information at: captaintom.net

'SpeedoMick' (pictured right) also known as Michael Cullen is another of my super-heros. Mick's walk during the winter of 2019/20 from John o' Groats to Land's End was truly epic. Not only did he do the

Picture used with kind permission granted by The SpeedoMick Foundation

walk in winter, which is pretty remarkable in itself, he did the walk wearing only his boots, hat, scarf, and his Speedo swimming trunks – hence his nickname. Mick is a well-known character on Merseyside, firstly as a dedicated Everton Football Club supporter often appearing in said minimalist clothing amongst the fans. Now he is not only known for his remarkable walk and previous lesser-known challenges, including an English Channel swim, all raising thousands of pounds in the process, but also for his challenging and difficult backstory, in other words his life before fame. SpeedoMick is a very different character to the Sir Tom we remember, but they have this in common: both have shared their own life experiences that we can all learn from and be inspired by. As I carry out my final checks to this manuscript during the last weekend of July 2021, SpeedoMick is somewhere in County Cork in southern Ireland, stomping along on his incredible 2,000-mile 'Giving Back Tour'. More information at: thespeedomickfoundation.org

My long solo walks started out in 1999 as personal holiday challenges; little more than escapism from my daily life working with computers; in the late 80s during my first career as an Architectural Technologist and continuing since 2000 as a self-employed IT consultant. This is one of the key reasons it has taken me so long to get round to writing a book, or hopefully, books about my walks. Now in semi-retirement with time on my hands I can tolerate actually using computers rather than fighting with them!

Here I must introduce my wife, Janine (Jan for short). Since the first of September 1984 she has been my undisputed and unchallenged 'basecamp manager'. Not just in terms of supporting me on long walks as the term suggests, but in every aspect of life. We have journeyed many places together as ordinary daily life presents them; and latterly, since 2002, as business partners. She is therefore fully qualified as official basecamp manager for my various walking activities over the years; indeed, it could be argued that Jan is responsible for this book.

I need to clarify; back in 1999 as I reached the tender age of forty, I got two notable birthday presents: my first mobile phone and a train ticket to Glasgow. Maybe after fifteen years of marriage she had finally had enough of this wily stick insect of a husband! I need not have worried. She was however clearly sending me away, on this occasion to walk the West Highland Way, my very first solo long-distance walk albeit of modest distance compared to more recent escapades.

This book, or these books as I am hoping they will become, are not walking guides, and are not intended to describe my bespoke routes in detail. Instead, using images and words, I attempt to paint a picture of what our island is like geographically, how varied the landscapes and places of habitation are, and give you some idea of what the true size of our island is; 'Sizing Up Great Britain' without a measuring tape!

I share my experiences; the pleasures the pains, thoughts, musings, chance encounters with people along the way and memorable conversations in the many pubs, cafes, and shops which pepper all of my walks; and the occasional rant (I have kept those to a minimum). As you journey with me you will also read about some of the amazingly kind people that accommodated me in all manner of unusual places from garden sheds and Scout hut storerooms to free-of-charge four-star hotel rooms and a Benedictine Monastery. My tent is always my backstop accommodation of need not want; some of the places I have stayed were truly lavish, and I loved it. What I can promise in these pages with absolute certainty is variety!

At a modest 80,823 square miles Great Britain is ninth in the global island land area league table. By way of comparison Madagascar is fourth with 226,658 square miles (nearly three times bigger than GB) and top of the list is Greenland which is just over ten times bigger at 822,700 square miles. We really are a modest rock compared with these super-giants. Nevertheless, I am hoping that you will travel with me on foot across the length and breadth of this modestly sized but beautiful island of ours and become convinced as I am that Britain, despite all that has happened in Parliament and elsewhere, is indeed still, genuinely, Great.

Why the apparent obsession with size you might ask? After all, 'size matters' is so last century and patently untrue in many settings. If, however, like me, you were born a few decades before the end of the last millennium, you might recall IBM's computing advert slogan: "Solutions for a small planet". From memory, I think they took a whole page in certain national newspapers in the late nineties, showing it below one of those famous images of Earth taken on one of the Apollo spaceflights. I really despised that advert. All of us understand that the world today is more accessible, both virtually and actually, than it has ever been in history; it is commonly said that 'the world is getting smaller'. Whilst I understand the expression and the commercial forces behind the advert, in principle I just do not buy it, because in reality we all know that it simply is not true…

Earth is huge. Granted, it is but a tiny pinprick in the vastness of space, but at a human level it is enormous; it always has been, and it always will be. My dislike of IBM's slogan was primarily because of one word: small. IBM may well have fantastic 'solutions', of that I have no doubt, but from my perspective the slogan smacked of arrogance and, at a subliminal level, for me bought into an unspoken secular agenda of trying to dump The Creator into the trashcan of history; an agenda that I and millions of others do not subscribe to… Make Earth smaller, make God smaller, make God go away.

As a Christian writer it is tempting to pepper this book with Biblical references, but I will not be doing this, nor will I be 'preaching' or getting too heavy and spiritual because I imagine that is not what you expect from this book. I will however quote one verse here which preferably should be read in context:

Romans 1 v 20

"For since the creation of the world God's invisible qualities - his eternal power and divine nature - have been clearly seen, being understood from what has been made, so that people are without excuse."

For my part I will let my journeys speak for themselves in words and pictures.

Come on, turn the pages, it's time to get our boots on - we need to get going!

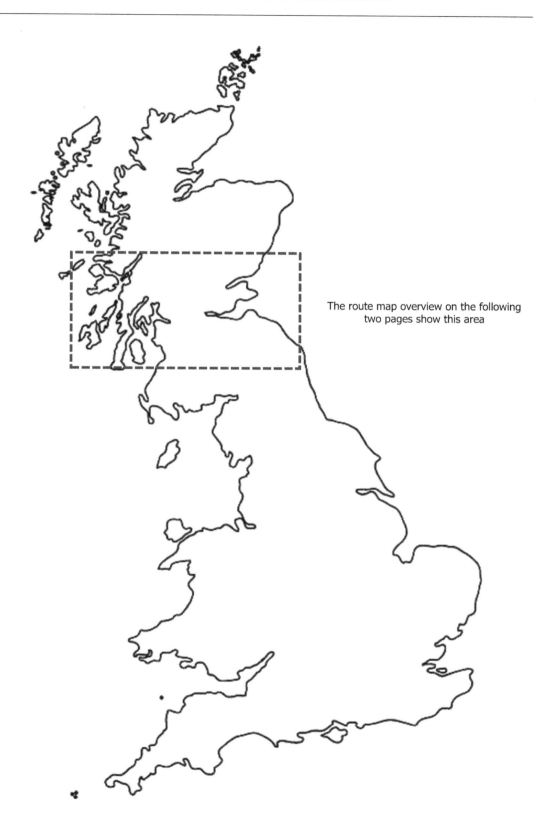

The route map overview on the following
two pages show this area

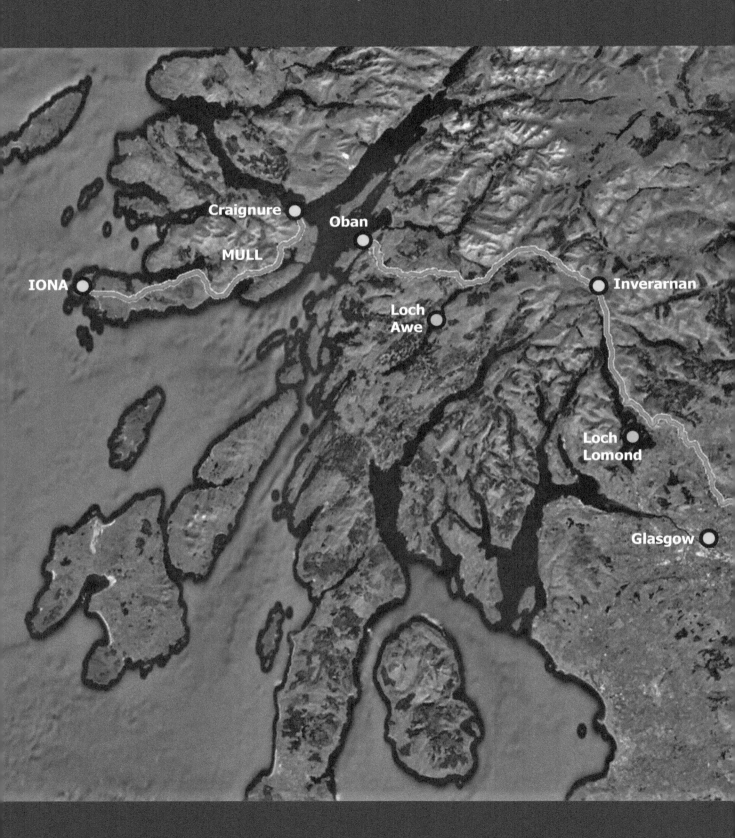

Bonnybridge

Edinburgh

LINDISFARNE

Traquair

PART ONE

Saints and Cheviots

Lindisfarne to Town Yetholm

Wednesday April 16, arrival day ● Lindisfarne

In the beginning there was Wainwright.

Alfred Wainwright (1907 – 1991) of English Lake District fame, also known as 'AW' to his many admirers, would have been the very last person to claim any deity-like status for himself, but he looms large in my psyche…

Standing on a tarmac road with the sea gently lapping onto your boots is not a thing that you can experience in many places in the British Isles, but that was a moment which was mine alone on Lindisfarne one still spring evening under a heavy leaden sky. It was Wednesday the 16th of April 2014. I was starting the first of what was to become a series of charitable walks across Great Britain.

Alfred Wainwright

Picture © copyright Derry Brabbs
used with kind permission

As I edged forward inch by inch, observing the occasional car making tentative moves forward to test the depth, I was more concerned whether I would get to Barn at Beal beyond the end of the causeway where I planned to camp that first night in enough light to see where to put my tent.

There is definitely no camping on Lindisfarne, but I simply had to start there properly, on the island, and then feel satisfied that I was abiding by one of Alfred Wainwright's key 'rules' for any long-distance journey; to have a properly defined start and finish. Something that I regard as really important for a satisfactory and fulfilling journey on foot.

Perryman's bus and St Mary's Church ~ both constitute transports of delight

Earlier I had caught a Perryman's bus in Berwick to get me onto Lindisfarne, also known as Holy Island, at around 1pm, and thereafter spent a few hours wandering around the tourist traps and eventually managing to grab a few quiet moments of contemplation in St Mary's Church as the hordes left in response to the advancing tide.

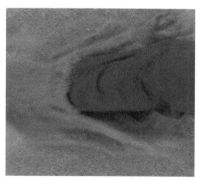

I was eager to get going so in fading light I made my way across The Links kicking my way through the powder-soft sand above the high-water mark heading west along the north coast of the island. All too soon I was leaving the sounds of the ocean behind.

Lindisfarne to Iona, a distance of around 300 miles, seemed to fulfil AW's criteria; his advice in the pages of his Coast-to-Coast guide to a walk across northern England was to "find your own way"; his walk being *a* way, not necessarily *the* way. On this basis I made my mind up not just about this walk, but all my future walks; they would all have a definite start and finish; well, that was my hope and intention.

Incidentally, I am aware that I was in no way a pioneer on this route having been beaten centuries earlier around 634AD by St Aidan, who is believed to have been the first to have made the journey on foot, albeit in the other direction and for quite different reasons.

St Aidan

I have been asked many times along the way on my walks whether I was on a pilgrimage…

I totally understand why I am asked this, but on all occasions my answer has amounted to 'no'. Some that know me would find this surprising, but whilst walking any distance is good for mind body and soul; spiritual matters, although of great importance to me, were not the only motivations behind these journeys. This does not mean that the walks did not provide 'soul food' or have spiritual aspects, both were present in good measure, but they are not my sole reasons for going on long solo walks. My main reasons are simple; I love walking long distances, the perspective of moving slowly, and being in beautiful places, although admittedly the latter are not so obviously evident on the outskirts of Galashiels or Glasgow! Other motivations are love of country and people in the patriotic sense, solitude, moments of silence, and what some might regard as a curious need for humility: Those moments when you realise just how small and insignificant you are compared to vast landscapes under an endless sky, sometimes facing dangerous weather and water – all potentially potent in the Highlands of Scotland.

Lindisfarne Causeway

The walk across the causeway was happily uneventful. Given more time daylight and patience I could have followed the poles on foot for a mile-and-a-half across the Holy Island Sands, but the official St Cuthbert's Way sticks to the road, so who was I to argue? It was just the excuse I needed; I have always been nervous about any chance of encountering quicksand, although I suspect that the speed of the tide hereabouts is a far greater hazard.

Lindisfarne Causeway (looking east)

I was 55 in 2014, and the idea of camping, particularly wild camping or 'roughing it' as some would call it, was beginning to lose its shine. The appeal which was strong in my younger years was fading. However, the freedom that backpacking brings is undeniable; and for me, setting out on a long walk without a tent packed in the rucksack on my back, would not feel right. I would almost feel naked; unpleasant indeed! So it was that I set my nine-year-old one-man tent down on the wet grass at Beal on that Wednesday evening out of necessity, not some weird desire to cocoon myself in a space not much bigger than a coffin. As is always the case on the first night in a bed that is other than the one you usually frequent, sleep was limited, and dawn seemed a very distant friend. My handwritten diary notes from Thursday morning suggest there were other factors bugging me on that first night: The tent sides that were taut only a few hours before now drooped all around, sopping wet within and without; sticking fly sheet and inner tent together as one.

Thursday April 17, day 1 ● Lindisfarne to Wooler

Within the confines of a small tent the waking up and getting moving experience has unique challenges expressed in moves and sounds that the human body is not ordinarily designed to make. For any observer of the human species, I imagine all would be regarded as noteworthy and deserving of investigation. Miraculously I was dry, but that was before I started the contortions of extracting myself from my mummified state and attempting to make myself presentable to the

Barn at Beal campsite

unseen world outside. This inevitably led to sleeping bag and other dry-critical items systematically mopping up the tent walls as said transformation proceeded. My carefully honed camping practices always evade me on day one.

As for my cooking skills or lack of them, let us not go there so soon in this book; that is a subject for much later by which time, hopefully, I will have earned your attention. I want you to keep reading, not abandon these pages to the shelf on the back of one encounter with my culinary adventures. It is time to move on, there is a long way to go...

With 18 miles to walk to Wooler and no desire to hang around I was away early, according to my notes at 7.30am, crossing the East Coast Main Line and the A1 in quick measure, safely negotiating both before nine. Mercifully, both were quiet, and I was soon making good progress following St Cuthbert's Way across the green Northumberland hinterland towards his cave. Disappointingly he wasn't in but there was plenty of evidence of those that had come after him.

East Coast Main Line

Woolly watchers

The A1 at Fenwick

Ancient cave, modern graffiti

At this early stage of the walk, I am in an archaeological paradise being in a part of Northumberland that is quite literally festooned with relics; ancient enclosures and settlements, cairns, cup, and ring marked rocks, forts and standing stones to name but a few. Suffice to say I am not an expert in any of this, but I could almost 'feel' their presence; history and time are not easily ignored.

In stark contrast to a timeless landscape the twenty-first century 'clever-tech' equipped walker can seem very out of place with all the modern navigational aids that many now regard as essential as a map and compass. The irony is of course that well-known manufacturers of so-called 'SatNav' (or sat-naff as my son used to call it) devices as used by walkers are never confident enough in their own technologies to say we can fully depend on them. We are still advised to take map and compass thereby defeating a key benefit of the technology - to help us travel lighter. I have to confess here and now that I have not always heeded that advice, although I never set off without a compass.

I spend many evenings during the winter preceding a walk meticulously planning every stage of a forthcoming journey with a high degree of cartographic accuracy. Being a bit of a map addict, this is no great hardship. In addition, because of my primary career in architectural building design;

St Cuthbert's Cave

getting things right in detail were pre-requisites of my daily working life so applying rigour to my route planning comes naturally and instinctively and is generally pleasurable, but patience is required, something I am not naturally gifted in. Accurate measurement of day-route distances was a pleasure of sorts; although sitting for prolonged hours staring at a screen, bearing in mind my second career of the last twenty years fixing computers and associated technologies, somewhat limits the enjoyment.

Looking west towards The Cheviot from the descent to Hetton Burn

During the planning stage I go through bouts of doubt and panic. Can I walk that far? Will there be a shop? Will that Ordnance Survey symbol indicating a pub actually exist and materialise into a bar serving a decent pint of bitter? Will there be food? Can I camp there? The latter question is an important consideration when planning a backpacking route anywhere in England and particularly in the English

Weetwood Bridge

home counties as traversed in later walks. These tosses and turns in emotions can swing between moments of impatience and anticipation of a seemingly distant date and the desire to don boots shoulder my rucksack and hit the trail, and moments when the thought of turning my back on home-comforts seems to be nothing short of folly. Eventually I have to decide; am I actually going to go? Usually, the question is answered by the purchasing of a train ticket or the booking of accommodation for the first night. Contemplating a life outside from the comfort of home has its consequences and is not really to be recommended.

Hereby ends the first of a few digressions. Where were we? Oh yes; heading across Weetwood Moor towards Wooler…

Weetwood Moor

I recall that apart from the odd shower that the day was largely dry, and the going underfoot was characteristically firm. Northumberland seems to bear the rain more graciously than my local Peak District hills to the east of Macclesfield, where they seem to need little excuse before becoming a boot-gripping quagmire. Northumberland is good underfoot.

Day one passed quickly and after a few pleasant hours of easy walking with only a couple of modest hill climbs I was in Wooler for my first time. A local café developed a sudden and powerful magnetic field the strength of a modest planet. Being the first eating establishment that I had seen since arriving in Berwick a couple of days earlier, it was impossible to resist. The pub could wait.

The Market Place Café had stalked its quarry and won, and it duly consumed me. There was less than a mile to go to camp two and it was only mid-afternoon, so haste was unnecessary, there was time to linger. If I find myself rushing on a walk something is going adrift. I remember a past incumbent vicar at my local church in Macclesfield describing what can often be needless rushing

Wooler ~ The Market Place Café is behind the post-box

around in our daily lives as 'hurry sickness'. From experience I know what he was getting at. That is the world that hopefully, for a few weeks at least, I am escaping from as I set out on a long walk. I think I ordered cheese and ham toasties and tea; I am rarely in the mood for complicated choices, and worse still, complicated food.

Duly satisfied and enjoying the late-afternoon sunshine I walked out of town to the local campsite at Highburn House. I like wild country, but I also like facilities; I can always do the former, but I always choose the latter if presented with the choice. My advancing years may not be a barrier, but they are a consideration.

The campsite owner directed me to the far corner of a beautifully mown sward of green away from the big tents and caravans, and on, as I later found out, a favoured grazing area as used by gangs of local ducks. Slightly oddly and not in accordance with what I regard to be good customer-facing practice, he drove across the site in his car, with me following on foot behind. Noted. Nice site though.

Friday April 18, day 2 ● Wooler to Town Yetholm

The second night was better than the first at Beal. It did not take much to be better but small mercies are always welcome. As I recall by morning the tent was significantly drier; not dry you understand just less wet. At a basic level I suppose I could attribute this to the fact that it didn't rain. Dew and internal moisture were at a minimum because of favourable mid-April temperatures. With inquisitive visitors speedily heading my way I ignited the Jetboil stove and disappeared inside my tent to celebrate all this with a breakfast of fruit and nut chocolate, dried fruit, and tea.

Jetboil presumably does not encourage use of their fabulous product inside a tent but sometimes I am forced to make exceptions. The biggest problem I get is condensation, but if that is all versus making a brew in the pouring rain, or as in this case defending yourself against the local wildlife, specifically militant ducks who were intent on invading my living space, then I know what to do; be careful and exercise that much derided thing called common-sense. I never change the gas canister inside the tent as that would be far too 'entertaining' and is definitely not good practice.

Just thirteen miles to walk today with Town Yetholm as the goal. A modest distance maybe but high ground of the northern Cheviot Hills lies between Wooler and the next camp, so after cleaning up my breakfast debris and being eager to get on the path I made an early start; the high moors were calling! Following St Cuthbert's Way, it is a lengthy and in places stiff climb from Wooler's back door to gain the moor top around Gains Law, well it's stiff if you are only on day two of a long trek and you are not particularly fit as I quickly realise that I am not when I set out. I get asked whether I 'train' ahead of a long walk; the short answer is no. Yes, I walk occasionally but in reality, I don't walk as much as I would like to; family life has its demands and members of said family are not convinced of the merits of yomping up and down hill and valley; especially over long distances and certainly not day after day.

It was a beautiful spring morning with just the right level of cooling breeze as I made my way across the moors towards Hethpool, happily striding forward in top gear accompanied by the song of moorland birds. Early day's enthusiasm can mean that despite my best efforts I never quite manage to pace myself as I should. It sounds crazy, but if I don't check myself, I can miss the whole point of moving through a landscape on foot; to go slowly, stop often, and look around as AW always advocated. With today's walk being only thirteen miles long I consciously tried to slow down. Another thing that happens early on in my walks is that I forget to think about where I am going; to perhaps consult the SatNav or maybe even a map once in a while.

The picture below reminds me of one such occasion. 'Take the fork to the right Paul, take the fork to the right…' says the small almost imperceptible voice in my head. In some kind of happy autopilot haze, I went left. I listened eventually, turning back beyond where the vehicle track rises.

Decisions, decisions ~ somewhere to the west of Gain's Law

The view to the south towards Cold Law from St Cuthbert's Way near Scaldhill

Descending to Hethpool and College Valley (above and below)

By eleven I am in Hethpool and just over halfway on the day's walk with another climb ahead up to the border fence. The sky became ever bluer, as if the flag of St Andrew were already waving in the heavens; it was a sign of things to come, decent weather would accompany me most of the way to Oban.

College Valley and Hethpool in the middle distance with the border hills beyond

College Valley and Hethpool

The first two climbs of any note had passed without incident except perhaps my heart being shocked into action upon realisation that I am actually serious about walking uphill with a modest fifteen kilograms on my back; some might say ill-advised for a man in his mid-fifties but hey, you only live once. All was well until after I crossed the border fence; this time nothing to do with my heart but everything to do with my head. Having lingered for twenty minutes or so at the border to ponder on its turbulent history and a future unknown, I bid a fond farewell to England and with some gusto and a sprinkling of happy giddiness I was off down the hill into Scotland.

Half-a-mile on I noticed. It was gone. My hat was no longer on my head, being brought to my attention by the even greater glare of the sun and my rapidly increasing head temperature. I was well on my way down at a brisk gravity-induced pace towards the appropriately named Green Humbleton before I realised. Humbled for the second time in less than four hours I was retracing my steps, this time not because of a wrong turn but because of an abandoned hat.

It was and still is a special hat: a Truswell Haulage branded cap given to me by one of their drivers in Macclesfield some weeks earlier, now rested on top of the fingerpost sign back up at the border. Suddenly the sky was not the only thing that was blue. I was mad at myself for having had another lapse in concentration. Back up the hill I went for what seemed more like a mile to say hello again to the country I thought I had left behind.

I am reminded here to say thanks to Truswell Haulage of Barnsley South Yorkshire for supplying hats for each of my charitable walks which, in my imagination as a 'backpacking haulier', had gained

A chance encounter in Macclesfield with Truswell Haulage ~ not often spotted west of the Pennines

status as a type of 'TrussyTrek' hallmark. I still like to wear one not just because of the family haulage connection but also because I now feel that my walking attire is incomplete without one; similar to walking without a full rucksack as mentioned earlier. Just a bit of fun really, and a little idiosyncrasy for the sake of photographs which I like. Next time you see a Truswell Haulage truck shout Trussy! …but don't expect a free hat.

'TrussyTrek' was a media-friendly name I used to use for my charitable walks, but no longer. Allow me to explain…

My schoolboy nickname was 'Trussy' and still is Trussy although all these fifty plus years later Janine hears it just as much as me because she is a Trussy as well. In fact, thinking about it, there are probably dozens of Trussies around the globe, as I imagine the Trussy nickname is readily given to any Truswell be they in Macclesfield or anywhere else. TrussyTrek grew out of my nickname of old and was first adopted for this walk as 'TrussyTrek 2014'. Why therefore have I dumped it into the dustbin of history? Basically, because I no longer like it, as it became a source of endless confusion and misappropriation. Local journalists in particular had the annoying habit of referring to my walk as '*The* TrussyTrek', as if it were the official name of some route or path, which it never has been, was never intended to be, and hopefully never will be. TrussyTrek was useful so I thought, for social media and on local radio, especially in the context of what became the first of my charity walks; a snappy one-word conjunction of two words being a fad of the time.

Scotland beckons ~ descending to the border wall and fence from Eccles Cairn

Taking five at the border

To an extent it worked, but not having any ambitions of social media or radio stardom I have now concluded it pointless and annoying so into the virtual bin it has gone. By all means call me Trussy, but please don't refer to my walk as TrussyTrek and definitely not *the* TrussyTrek. I digress…

With cap firmly replaced on head I was soon down in the Halterburn Valley and on the road for a short mile in the company of the Pennine Way climbing the "cruellest hill of all" as AW referred to it in his 'Pennine Way Companion'. I was on the lookout for weary Pennine Wayfarers nearing the end of their quest; there were none to be seen, I was too early. The last day of the Pennine Way if done in one go as described by AW is the longest and most arduous since leaving Edale.

Signs of progress

St Cuthbert's Way and the Pennine Way share the same route into Kirk Yetholm

I had mixed feelings as I sat down at the Border Inn of Pennine Way and Wainwright fame. I had a couple of attempts at walking the UK's oldest National Trail many years earlier as a keen but green walker in my late teens; on the first occasion not getting beyond Malham, and on the second running out of time in Bellingham; and, if truth be known, I seem to remember a bus was involved on that latter occasion. Well put it like this; I recall being in Dufton on the west side of the Pennines and Alston, England's highest market town, on the east side, but I have no recollection of any walking in between and can say with absolute certainty that I have never trod the high way from Great Dunn Fell to Cross Fell. Well not yet anyway.

Perhaps I am too readily self-critical about my early forays out on to the hills. Of course, way back then I was not alone, I had friends with me; I was keen, they were less so. Also, the gear we carried was not in any way lightweight and was of limited quality. Quantity yes, quality no. Blisters were big and mighty; patience was in short supply. These were my formative years on the hills; their effect on me was positive for the long term. They are distant memories lost in the haze of early adulthood, but precious nonetheless.

Here we take a break from my walking recollections to admire the work of the man that I very briefly introduced on page sixteen: Alfred Wainwright (AW).

Reproduced here (with the kind permission of The Estate of A. Wainwright © copyright) is page 5 of AW's 'Pennine Way Companion' which shows the final section of England's best-known National Trail. The Pennine Way starts in Edale 19 miles ESE of Manchester and ends 270 route miles north in the Scottish Borders' village of Kirk Yetholm.

AW was not a fan of the Pennine Way, but you would not know that from a cursory glance at his work, each page showing the same attention to detail and mastery of pen and ink that made his Pictorial Guides to the Lakeland Fells so famous.

He described his guides as "love letters" and it easy to see why. They are truly remarkable works of art. He did not describe the Pennine Way Companion in those terms but the same dedication to task is evidenced on every page.

Like many walkers I am an admirer of all AW's work, most of his books taking pride of place on my bookshelves. He continues to inspire myself and generations of walkers both in this country and beyond these shores, and I therefore dedicate this page to Alfred Wainwright's lasting memory in this year of 2021 thirty years after his passing.

Look carefully on the reproduced page for the words "cruellest hill of all". (you might need a magnifying glass!) This photograph shows the hill AW was describing, which climbs the road out of the Halterburn Valley as I saw it on my descent from the border.

I am a proud member of the Wainwright Society.

More information at wainwright.org.uk

BURNHEAD TO KIRK YETHOLM

1" Ordnance Sheet 70

Kirk Yetholm would seem a lovely village to anyone who had walked 270 miles to reach it even if it were slums and slagheaps. But in fact it *is* a lovely village: its setting in a pleasant valley is enhanced by trim cottages around a green, an attractive inn, an old pinnacled church and a quiet but friendly atmosphere. In former times it was a meeting place and camping ground for an ancient clan of gipsies, and traces of their occupation remain.

Today it is a peaceful sanctuary, its main link with the busier world beyond being the bus service to Kelso.

Kirk Yetholm
Youth Hostel
Border Hotel — WOOLER
270
400
Kirk — to ← STOP! This is the end. Son, you have walked the Pennine Way.
Shop — 100 yards to go.
30 m.p.h. sign. SLOW DOWN!
KELSO
400 yards to go — raspberries on the roadside — chalet — first view of Kirk Yetholm. At last!
500 — The road climbs 150 feet from the cattle grid — the cruellest hill of all. Get up off your knees. Don't give in. The agony will soon be over.
600
barn
Take a last long look back
Staerough Hill is on this side
1200 yards to go
1300 yards to go
1400 yards to go
1500 yards to go
269 — cattle grid
mushrooms on the road verges

The last geography lesson:
The hills around are the northern outliers of the Cheviots and all their streams escape to the north, joining Bowmont Water on its way to the River Tweed via the River Till. Staerough Hill is the last height of note; beyond, across the valley in which lie the villages of Kirk Yetholm and Town Yetholm, are low foothills and the wide strath of the Tweed at Kelso.

barn — ← The banks of the stream are fringed with musk, a plant more associated with domestic gardens.

Halterburn Hotel

The Halterburn Hotel is a welcome surprise. Formerly this building was a deserted farmhouse but a few years ago it was converted to a comfortable and modern hotel. As the first place of refreshment after 27 inhospitable miles its appeal to walkers with spectacular thirsts and appetites is irresistable. There are beds, too.

Kirk Yetholm out of sight in the next valley

Staerough Hill

the last climb (road to Kirk Yetholm)

road
Halter Burn — Halterburn Hotel (in trees)
268
cattle grid

chalet
sheds

Burnhead (farm)

Burnhead

The Halterburn Valley

Positively the last lap. Honestly.

7

The Border Hotel at Kirk Yetholm

I had to learn how to enjoy being in wild places, most of the time we are indoor creatures so it can take practice. Those early walks in my late teens and early twenties did however serve to energise my appetite for the great outdoors, but then 'music' (I use the term loosely) came along. Guitars, bands, and girls were my spare time pre-occupation in the eighties. The hills had to wait, fortunately for me they were not going anywhere anytime soon.

Choosing from the Border Inn menu I settled on a pint of bitter and fish n chips; soon to become my default order in any pub where food was available. Time passed by chatting to a couple sat at a picnic bench in the beer garden; one pint of Bishop Neame Spitfire became two, and just as I am convincing myself I'd done enough walking for the day I remembered I was in the wrong Yetholm, my plan was to be in Town not Kirk.

AW was keeping a close eye on me as I returned my glass to the bar. In the pages of his books, he was always keen to encourage his readers to stick to goals in life whether on the path or elsewhere. I therefore nodded respectfully and dutifully in AW's direction, paid my dues at the bar remembering that AW had long since stopped the practice of 'charge it to Wainwright'. In any case I didn't qualify, I was on the wrong walk, not that anyone could have guessed apart perhaps from being too clean. I shouldered my rucksack for the last mile of the day.

Entering Town Yetholm, I had the first clue that I was adapting to life as a solitary walker. Well, when you see someone struggling to cut sheet plywood on a pair of wobbly trestles what do you

Bowmont Water separates the two Yetholms

Town Yetholm

do? There is great freedom in walking alone, but I am not naturally a solitary person, I soon seek out company and conversation after a few hours solo walking. I like solitude but in limited doses.

Shortly after crossing the bridge over Bowmont Water, I found myself gripping the rough edge of a half-inch plywood sheet outside the campsite owner's garage in Town Yetholm. Secretly and somewhat selfishly I was hoping that my help might have earned me an offer of internal accommodation under a proper roof but to no avail. Within the hour I was digging the tent out for my third night under ripstop nylon. Like I said, I camp out of necessity not choice; in any case it was a gorgeous evening. It was good to be outside on what turned out to be an excellent riverside campsite.

Town Yetholm is pleasant although you get the impression that despite its superior size, it lives a little in the shadow of the village next door. Becoming the official end of the first National Trail

Camp 3 at Kirkfield Caravan Park

Bowmont Water

Town Yetholm

does earn you a certain kudos, deserved or not. The wide main street is very agreeable with terraced houses all of individual character keeping watch over the comings goings, and a beady eye on those odd-looking characters with large bags on their backs.

Consumption of an early evening pint accompanied by a couple of highland measures of single malt was in order and was all I needed to send me drifting off into dreamland under that ever-deepening blue sky. I went in search of said refreshment at The Plough Hotel and was away by 9pm. Thankfully, I managed to find my tent and not embarrass myself by trying to enter anything that was vaguely tent shaped as happened some years earlier…

Back in 1999 on the West Highland Way there was such an incident just north of Loch Lomond after a long evening in the Inverarnan Hotel (now renamed The Drovers Inn). I have fuzzy recollections of joyfully staggering back to the Beinglas campsite late in the evening and trying to enter several tents that were not mine. I am not a recreational drinker, which means I don't need much to become pleasantly befuddled, especially when enlivened by a good day on the hills. However, it helps to remember that Scottish measures of single malt are more generous than those south of the border. Thankfully on this particular evening, mine was the only small tent in town. I'd need more than the modest quantity consumed in The Plough to confuse a caravan with my tent!

Kirkfield Caravan Park was delightful; one of the nicest sites I have ever stayed on as a backpacker. Places primarily intended for accommodation on wheels are not typically so welcoming and pleasant, in fact sometimes you can feel like an intruder intent on holding noisy all-night parties and getting generally rowdy. Rarely a problem with backpackers in my experience, especially solo ones whose first priority is usually to turn in as soon as daylight fades.

PART TWO

St Cuthbert's is one Way the Southern Uplands another

Town Yetholm to Traquair

Saturday April 19, day 3 ● Town Yetholm to the Eildon Hills

Morning broke with that characteristic crisp chill of an April morning. Yes, there is the promise of a good day ahead but first you have got to get there, usually involving a degree of discomfort as you try to persuade your tired body out of broken slumber and sleeping bag and into the cold morning air. I was up at 5.30am; and in contrast to the previous morning the tent was as stiff as cardboard. Time to fire up the JetBoil and get the brew on! Porridge? Well sometimes. It takes me a few days of 'acclimatisation' before I start cooking food as well. Time to shake the ice off the tent and get going – food can wait!

Wideopen Hill beckons; a modest height of less than 400 metres, but with views back to the Yetholms nestling in the Bowmont Valley that are just gorgeous, it really is a gem, especially on a sparkling morning like this with so much of the route to come. As I climbed, I did not know just how long this day was going to be. Today was going to be exceptional, but not necessarily for all the right reasons.

On the way up Crookedshaws Hill I had my first encounter with what I term 'militant sheep'. You know the sort, the sort that stand their ground rather than scarper at the first sight of a human as you would ordinarily expect. I had no idea what they were munching, whatever it was it seemed to be bolstering them with defiance and courage. I kept my distance; upsetting militant sheep had the potential to spoil my day.

Crookedshaws Hill

Militant sheep

Looking back down Crookedshaws Hill towards Yetholm Loch and the Bowmont Valley

Up ahead the bright green ground continued its rise into the blue, with views opening up all around particularly to the north and west across the Teviot and Tweed valleys towards today's destination, the one I had planned, or so I thought, near Newtown St Boswells. Looking back to the west of the Yetholms and Yetholm Law (in this context 'Law' is a Scots word meaning hill) I picked out a small patch of silvery blue; first loch of the trip: Yetholm Loch!

Just occasionally I am pleased with my photography, at the top of this page is one such example. It must be said that of all the influence people have had on a landscape, surely the drystone walls of this island are amongst the most wondrous to behold. Hence the recognition of my son-in-law's skill in the acknowledgements on page three. I mean look at it. Yes, essentially this is a landscape fashioned and shaped by centuries of farming, but was there ever something that looks just so right? Build it in clay bricks and you would not be so convinced.

With extensive views all around and not another soul to be seen apart from a few sheep keeping an eye on my every move, I lingered on the top of Wideopen Hill and took too many photographs. Is digital photography liberation or laziness I ask myself? Whatever your opinion, on this occasion I was pleased to not have to worry about the cost of film and developing as in times gone by, plus the uncertainty of the results. Strangely I miss that aspect of film photography.

Extensive views from Wideopen Hill

Today I really could not fail; the views from the top of the appropriately named Wideopen Hill are just that; wide open; amazing in fact, and a classic example of something I have discovered over the years; height does not necessarily mean extensive where big views are concerned. At 368 metres (1,207 feet in old money) this is no mountain but what it lacks in stature it certainly makes

up for in the vistas department. Definitely worth the climb, don't let the sheep put you off. The St Cuthbert's Way notice on the fence at the top of the hill states "This is the highest point of the Way and also the halfway point between Melrose and Lindisfarne". Today I was to walk further in a day than I had ever done before covering more miles than days 1 and 2 combined. The day was not planned that way it just happened…

Accompanied by my shady companion I was soon descending again to the road alongside the Kale Water (stream not lake) towards the interestingly named village of Morebattle. With my grasp of British history as a whole being shall we say, tentative, I hereby defer to Wikipedia:

"The place-name comes from the Anglian (language) mere-bōðl – 'dwelling place by the lake' (Linton Loch). No evidence of any battles (the simplistic origin) exists."

Morebattle with a first glimpse of the Eildon Hills in the far distance

Disappointingly it seems the place name has absolutely nothing to do with battles. Apparently, the name is rooted in old Anglian and loosely translates as "dwelling place by the lake". Quite where or why the lake has gone is unclear, but it seems likely that the area was drained as part of 19th century agricultural improvements. One mile to the east of the village Ordnance Survey mapping indicates the location of Linton Loch as mentioned in the Wiki page but marked on the map as marshy ground with a couple of small ponds.

As it happens that is not the end of this day's curiosities (and it is only mid-morning). Not only does Morebattle have less battle and in fact none at all, by way of compensation it does have the delightfully named Teapot Street which, according to local legend, was named by Sir Walter Scott:

...who, passing through the village one day, noticed the wives in the street carrying teapots to the nearby Kale Water to picnic, and remarked, "that must be Teapot Street."

Aside from legends, true or not, Morebattle is a tidy quiet place; well, it was on this particular Saturday morning where a compulsory stop for an overdue breakfast was in order. Armed with two bananas a large apple and an orange drink I installed myself on a conveniently located bench outside the village shop, duly consuming all before setting off on the road towards Cessford and its castle.

April is a transitional month across all of the British Isles, and you feel those transitional shifts in the weather more north of the border than anywhere else. At this stage of what has now become a walk across Scotland I am still a long way from the Highlands where you can encounter both blizzards and heatwaves at this time of year. Here in the Scottish Borders were no such extremes; but as I sat basking in the morning sunshine it was not lost on me that only a few hours earlier I had been shaking ice off my tent. The warmth was intoxicating and delicious; it would have been easy to doze off into slumber land.

St. Cuthbert's Way follows the road west out of Morebattle towards Cessford. Since leaving Lindisfarne the Way has on the whole been particularly good at avoiding roads. I have nothing against road walking in principle, in fact sometimes I quite enjoy it because of the ease of navigation and the knowledge that you are far less likely to encounter herds of excitable bovines, which are a constant concern at this time of year. Providing they are reasonably quiet it is a good way to make unhindered progress through agricultural pastures, although serenity on the roads and lanes of England and Scotland cannot be guaranteed and you must always have your wits

Cessford and its Castle

about you. It only takes one bad driver and a lapse in concentration for things to go seriously wrong.

Cessford's 15th century castle soon came into view. At first it is seen as an insignificant box-like structure on the near horizon, but as you get closer it looms large and becomes quite imposing in the otherwise gently rolling landscape. Situated in an elevated position, on top of a gentle rise just to the east of the few houses and large farm that make up the hamlet of Cessford, it doesn't seem to have any strategic importance; other than perhaps being a place for holding forces between more significant settlements, such as Floors Castle to the north at Kelso, or maybe Ferniehirst Castle to the south of Jedburgh. Don't quote me; I am not pretending any expertise here, all just interested speculation on my part.

Neatly set in their surroundings and in one row, the few houses at Cessford look like escapee miner's cottages from across the border in Northumberland, although the dormer windows facilitating light into the cleverly concealed upper storey do give them that distinctly Scottish look and modest scale. Built in local stone like the walls seen earlier on Wideopen Hill they fit the landscape perfectly.

Easy walking on a mix of road and farm tracks through pleasant countryside characterises St

Passing place sign on the road to Crailing ~ a sure sign of Scotland

Cuthbert's Way between Cessford and Jedfoot Bridge. Hereabouts I had a rare encounter with a couple of backpackers heading east. Even on established routes like this one I rarely see other walkers, even less so backpackers. There are exceptions like on the West Highland Way which as mentioned in the introduction was my first long solo walk. Such is its popularity that quiet solitude can become a scarce thing, although I was lucky on that occasion and saw hardly anyone from Milngavie to Fort William; perhaps due to the foul weather that accompanied me most of the way.

At the end of a short section of road to the south-east of Crailing I saw my first passing place sign. Such signs are seen all over Scotland and in particular generous measure north of the Great Glen and have almost iconic status. Well, they do in my mind. Sadly, they are gradually disappearing from the primary routes where they used to be as common as they still are on minor rural roads. Many of the more heavily trafficked arteries now widened to afford easy passage for ever increasing numbers of motorhomes on established leisure drives like the Scottish 'North Coast 500'. I have no objection to any of this, but it does seem that the old idea of mystery tours and a spirit of adventure is being lost. Here I reference Wainwright and his advice to "find your own way". Perhaps the benefit to local trade and communities along such routes outweighs what some might perceive as fanciful romantic nonsense and an unwillingness to move on. Personally, I used to enjoy the slow progress

Monteviot Bridge and a sign of the times

along the old roads; more time to stop and look around; another Wainwright principle, whether on wheels or on foot. Not sure how much you can take in at 60mph. Scotland is like its most famous export; it should be savoured slowly.

Beyond Monteviot Bridge and stately house of the same name things got interesting; the day was to become longer; significantly longer. In blissful ignorance of what was to come I stopped at the Woodside Plant Centre & Birdhouse Tearoom for a bite to eat at about 3pm (nice food, no birds) anticipating an early wild camp at the interestingly named Divet Ha' Wood which is en route a few hundred yards north. Thereabouts I reached my daily target of around 18 miles and accordingly had planned a stop in my itinerary. I remember some months earlier struggling with the planning of this one but having reckoned that a wild camp much further along the route towards Newtown St Boswells would have been less desirable, I reckoned one night in what looked like a quiet patch of woodland would be the best option. I was wrong. Aside from putting my tent on the path, the hoped-for clearing with suitable patch of springy green turf did not materialise. The ground round about was strewn with a thick layer of spiky tree detritus; about as uninviting as you can get.

The Afternoon was only half done so with unbroken blue skies above and with some apprehension, I pressed on. I never like deviating from my accommodation plan because of the knock-on effect that can have on a long walk, but on this occasion, it was necessary that I did. I was on the line of the ancient Roman Road called Dere Street so at least I knew than the route ahead to Newton would be straight.

About half-a-mile beyond the woods I had my second encounter of the day with another walker, who seemed to be in a hurry, although granted; he was significantly younger than me. We got chatting about my camping plans (or lack of them) and he suggested that a camp by the river near Maxton, about 4 miles further on, could be a possibility. Enlivened by this prospect I got marching, Roman military-fashion. Typically for a Roman Road, views left, and right were excellent, although again not because of great elevation but because of just enough height above the adjacent landscapes.

Divet Ha' Wood

Another interruption to my progress was soon upon me. Unknowingly I was on the site of the Battle of Ancrum Moor which Wikipedia tells me was:

> "…fought during the War of the Rough Wooing in 1545."

I like the 'rough wooing' bit. Unbeknown to me such a thing was possible but there you go. Clearly Henry VIII's ambitions for his son Edward in a hoped-for union with the infant Mary Queen of Scots knew no boundaries! Unfortunately for Henry on that 27th February day in 1545 with a loss of some 800 combatants and 1,000 prisoners held by his enemies, this day put an end to his English incursions in the Scottish border lands.

I thought I was looking at an old but rather handsomely made grave. Whilst it drew my attention mainly because of its isolated and somewhat lonely location, I took a few snaps and moved on; I was more eager to find the anticipated patch of green by that river; so much so that I completely ignored the plaque which is so clearly visible in one of the resulting pictures. Let us take a moment to remember Fair Maiden Lilliard by reading this short text from the plaque:

Lilliard's Stone

> "Fair maiden Lilliard
>
> Lies under this stane
>
> Little was her stature
>
> But muckle was her fame
>
> Upon the English loons
>
> She laid monie thumps
>
> an' when her legs were cuttit off
>
> She fought upon her stumps."

Lilliard is said to have fought at the battle following the death of her lover.

By the time I doffed my hat and bid farewell to the Fair Maiden the sun was getting worryingly low in the sky, so resuming said military determination I shifted into turbo top gear and thumped west along the road at a steady heady speed of 3½ mph. I reckon my true average across a whole route is below three so that is some going! By now I was getting my first proper views of the Eildon Hills which overlook Melrose, but even 'as the crow flies'

they still looked an awfully long way away and because St Cuthbert's Way develops a rebellious streak after the constraining straight line of the Roman Road it is further than you might reasonably imagine.

Beyond Maxton the Way stubbornly follows the sinuous curves of the River Tweed adding miles to the route. With hindsight and noting the hour of the day plus what came later, I perhaps should have ignored the seductive curves and wooded beauty of the riverside in favour of continuing along Dere Street, which beyond Forest Lodge becomes the busy A68. In true militaristic fashion I could have saved at least two miles by following that direct into Newton St Boswells, although again referencing the Romans they would not have had the exciting prospect of being flattened by a forty-ton artic or some other wheeled monster.

Walkway down to the riverside from Maxton

Arriving at the riverside it quickly became apparent that I was in dog-walking country. This was not the idyllic wild camping opportunity that I had hoped for. I may have missed the spot that the speedy young walker had in mind, but I just was not comfortable with putting my tent down anywhere on this riverside land; a brief exchange with a local dog-walker did not help matters. Words were along the lines of "…the landowner isn't friendly…" That was all the hint I needed; plans for a night by the river were hurriedly ditched and needless panic set in. Needless because I was hardly in bandit country, but wherever I walk, whether in England or in Scotland, I do my utmost to follow the law of the land I am privileged to explore. The Law in Scotland is quite different to that in England, and in many ways much more relaxed about wild camping; but in areas such as this, a long way from the usual haunts of backpackers in wild country, asking the landowner's permission is a reasonable prerequisite before laying your head down for the night on their land.

Beyond Mertoun Bridge the riverside meadow is quite wide at Great Stenhouse but with Saint Boswells Golf Club land overlooking it again it just did not feel right, and so I continued around another long bend in the river at Dryburgh Abbey which seemed to take forever to negotiate and

River Tweed at Mertoun Bridge

then finally I made my way up into town. By this time daylight was fading fast, and I was spending more time on my phone using it for actual phone calls back to 'basecamp' rather than for taking photographs. Back home Janine was digging around online to see if there was any possibility of accommodation in Bowden a mile-and-a-half west from Newton, whether that be a place to camp or B&B. A night on the

Warm evening sunshine on Mertoun Bridge

hills was quickly becoming the only option although to get there I would have to climb in the dark.

For the first time since leaving Lindisfarne I deviated from the official St Cuthbert's Way and walked along the B6398 road which was mercifully quiet, thereby avoiding a potentially tricky walk in the dark alongside Bowden Burn. Janine called back; nothing was available. It was time to turn on the head torch and find my way onwards and upwards. By the time I reached Bowden I had walked further in a single day than I had ever done before having gone way

Sunset over the Eildon Hills

past my previous personal record of 25 miles. I was feeling properly tired, but when I finally accepted that I was going to have to push on, and that I was at least guaranteed an undisturbed and legal wild camp on the Eildon Hills, I had one of those curious waves of energy out of nowhere. I had not eaten anything substantial since my mid-afternoon café break, which seemed many more hours ago than the five that had elapsed as I opened the gate onto the hills from Feuars Park in Bowden, a village I never saw.

Back on the official St Cuthbert's Way route all unnecessary fears and apprehensions disappeared as guided by torchlight I made my way up the Eildon Mid Hill flanks through Broad Wood. If anything, I experienced an almost schoolboy-like sense of adventure.

Sometimes my walk planning is my Achilles heel. In my mission to manage my daily miles I probably go over the top and micro-manage myself too much. My plan to camp in the woodland north of the café was a failure and a good example of the risks involved when trying to judge what a place will be like sat in front of a computer. Ordnance Survey mapping is excellent in every way, but one must always bear in mind that lines and symbols on paper (or screen) is one thing; the reality can be very different.

The bright lights of Galashiels and Melrose from camp 4

Moon rising over camp 4

It was about 11pm by the time I fumbled with rucksack and unfurled nylon on top of the thick springy heather into something that I hoped was vaguely tent shaped. I had walked 31 miles from Town Yetholm. A personal record that was set more by accident than design.

My short overnight location was high up on the west side of Eildon Hill North below the dip in the hills that I had seen the sun set behind a few hours earlier, looking down on the twinkling lights of Melrose far below with Galashiels in the distance. Progress was slow in the dark but somehow, I had managed to stay on route. It was the first time that I had hiked somewhere unfamiliar in the dark; I was exhausted but quite pleased with myself.

Relieved and exceedingly tired I tumbled into my tent; and then out again. Let's just say it wasn't level. I am not talking slightly sloping as good camping practice stipulates to avoid sleeping in puddles, I mean properly at an angle. By torchlight it looked okay but once inside gravity took control. I think I spent much of the night curled in a foetus-like bundle in the bottom half of the tent. Sleep was shallow and fleeting, but somehow just about possible. Maybe it was the soothing thumps of the disco drifting up from the town far below that did the trick.

I was in the tent for five hours at most. My diary notes tell me that I was writing them at 4.20am and that I was concerned about a sudden episode of arrythmia that I experienced as soon as I got settled. With hindsight, it is hardly surprising that the old ticker was having a bit of a 'fit' suddenly stopping as I did after a very long day. Perhaps it was responding to the sounds of the distant disco beats; certainly that is how it felt in my chest as my heart bopped popped and boogied against my ribcage, in and out of time with the rhythm.

Most of us experience palpitations as part of normal everyday life but they can get scary. Thankfully in my case I have received specialist advice telling me that they are not anything to be unduly concerned about, although that advice came some months after and prompted by my experience on this walk. Arrythmia was a concern to different degrees for the whole of this walk but particularly over the first few nights when in typically male fashion it became a worry; during the day it was never a problem; well not one I noticed.

Sunday April 20, day 4 ● Eildon Hills to Traquair

Freezing camp 4 on the Eildon Hills

Morning revealed a frozen tent set at a jaunty angle amongst the heather. Looking inside the the groundsheet had a profile reminiscent of a dentist's chair. Quite how I slept at all I have no idea; needs must I suppose. It had been a very cold night. Once the disco had subsided all became quiet despite the hilltop breeze. That was because the tent was as stiff as a board, once again frozen solid. The last time I remember the tent being frozen like that was at Sligachan on Skye back in the late eighties when camping with Janine, but we were young and in love so staying warm was not a problem. This time I had the less romantic solution of thick socks, duck-down jacket, and beany inside my sleeping bag; no substitute of course for my wife's company though I don't think she would have enjoyed this particular location. Janine is adventurous to a point, but she is also well grounded unlike her seemingly unhinged husband.

Once again it was time to shake the ice off the tent. As I found out in subsequent walks dealing with early morning ice is common in April, but somehow you don't expect it even though you know it is totally normal, particularly in Scotland, where spring is perceptibly later than south of the border. It is in fact possible to rid the tent of more water when frozen, it all depends how energetic you are feeling and how keen you are to reduce weight. Just give it a good shake and you're done. Despite daylight the air seemed to be getting colder, so I did not linger on the hillside although a call of nature had to be answered first which was when the first equipment failure of the trip occurred; the toilet trowel broke. "How crap was that!" declares my diary. I promise I left no visible evidence of my stay. Enough information already…

Woolly escapee watchers

Melrose boot cleaning facility

I decamped as quickly as I could shaking the tent madly and, in a frenzy of movement, scrunched the tent into my rucksack. No careful folding and rolling around the poles this morning. On checking my fingers were attached to my hand but with every passing second handling the freezing fabric was resulting in a worrying lack of feeling in my fingertips. I am sure I was a long way from developing frostbite, but it didn't feel that way. I hauled on my rucksack and bounced through the heather down to the path which I had strayed some yards away from in the dark. In half-an-hour I was back down in civilisation climbing the steps between houses onto Dingleton Road and on into Melrose.

Clean your boots first though! A householder had gone to the trouble of providing boot cleaning facilities with a sign reading as follows: *"When the ground is muddy use the scraper to clean your boots. Please do not muddy the steps.*

Thank you."

To the householder I say full marks and a hearty well-done for taking practical action.

Grey overcast skies were the order of the day as I adjusted to the town's surroundings. It was still very early on a Sunday morning and as a result there were few people around, so I found a bench by the abbey and sat down to take stock, grab a bite to eat from my dwindling supplies and sort out the rucksack chaos I caused earlier. It was very tempting to go horizontal and grab some sleep, but I thought better of it.

As the photograph overleaf (taken by a kind and sympathetic passer-by) confirms, I felt and looked jaded. I am glad I stayed awake, had I drifted off into dreamland I think I could have kissed

Melrose Abbey

goodbye to making any further progress that day. I had a walk in the grounds of Melrose Abbey where, as evidenced by piles of scaffolding in a few places, maintenance and restoration works were taking place, and then got on my way. Only a modest 19 miles to do today to my first rest day at Quair View B&B in Traquair. That was motivation enough to shift me off that bench.

Melrose Abbey marks the official start of St Cuthbert's Way which ends on Lindisfarne, but it wasn't until I got to the Gattonside Chain Bridge that I realised I had completed this first significant section of the walk. I had been far too busy sorting out my rucksack to notice.

It was a good feeling to be joining a familiar route once again. I walked the Southern Upland Way in 2005 albeit in the opposite direction. The chain bridge across the River Tweed which takes the 212-mile route north to Lauder was familiar even though I had only seen it once before. On that occasion I had well over two-thirds of the route behind me, on this occasion the reverse was true. The Southern Upland Way was and still is a tough route particularly in the western half, so I knew what the upcoming eastern section to Traquair via the magnificent Three Brethren cairns and the

Gattonside Chain Bridge

A familiar sign shelter indicates that I had
joined the Southern Upland Way

The River Tweed at Gattonside

lofty Old Drove Road was like; one of the very best on that walk and one that I intended to enjoy after the rigours of yesterday. First though I had some negotiating to do; someone was building a railway on my route.

The Southern Upland Way crosses the River Tweed on the railway bridge. Back in 2005 this was one part of the dismantled Borders Railway between the towns of Galashiels and Melrose. In 2014 it was a building site. Accidentally but still on the official route I found myself on the wrong side of the site security fence and had to be rescued; literally, as I could not escape the six-foot-high Herras fencing that was keeping me in unwilling captivity. Thankfully, a local saw me and knew a weak spot in the defences and was able to let me out; without his assistance I would have ended up retracing my steps adding two miles to the day and further expletives to my public vocabulary.

Site-seeing on the new Borders Railway

After yesterday's epic 31 miles I was in no mood for diversions!

I was relieved to have escaped. A railway soon to be alive with trains again can only be a good thing; quite why it was closed in the first place only a certain Dr Beeching could answer. Surely in 1969 Galashiels and Melrose were overlooked? Their need for a railway connection to the capital seems pretty obvious today; clearly it was not so obvious back then; or more likely ignored.

The unforgiving hard surfaces of the embryonic railway and the brief encounter with urban tarmac was taking its toll. I was starting to limp. I could feel I was developing the mother of all blisters on my right heel and action would soon be needed in the form of a little grit-your-teeth wayside surgery.

Having admired the local sewage works and won freedom from the railway construction site, I was once again diverted off route and found myself in a housing estate wandering along Woodstock Avenue in the Langlee area of Galashiels. I found my way off the estate and back across the railway on a footbridge that put me almost in academia land at Heriot-Watt University Scottish Borders campus. The change in environment that I was experiencing only a few hours after a frozen hilltop camp was mind-numbing. At least my hands felt alive again as I madly shoved buttons on the GPS. It was only 10am but I knew I had a long way to go to get to the promised land of a day off; I was going to need it. Every step was a painful one, so I was eager to find my way out of town and back onto the hills so that I could attend to the offending object under my

Woodstock Avenue, Galashiels

right foot. I got back on route and headed for Galashiels Academy as quickly as my limping style would permit. I could remember the school distinctly from 2005 as being the abrupt welcome and unusual entrance into suburbia when walking east on the Southern Upland Way (will initialise 'SUW' from hereon)

My memories of 2005 were not as complete as I thought they were because I had forgotten that the encounter with suburbia at the Academy is a brief one, as the eastbound SUW heads away from Galashiels almost as soon as it arrives, heading back on to open country at Gala Hill. In my westerly direction it was with some relief that I found my way up onto the hill behind Netherbarns to a conveniently located seat that, unknown to the good folks of Galashiels and Melrose, I have named 'Hospital Bench'.

'Hospital Bench'

It was time to deploy the Compeed (other blister repair solutions are available but take my word for it — these are the best) but first there was a really icky-tricky bit of preparation to do. I will not get into too much detail here. I have in fact already shown mercy to you dear reader by not including a photograph of my wayside d.i.y. 'surgery'. "A picture is worth a thousand words" so it is said, in this case and in the context of this book that would have been a thousand too many!

Let us just say that liquid pressure had to be relieved, raw new skin exposed, skin trimmed and affected area <u>dried</u>. Thereafter take aim and slap it on, smoothing all edges down and pressing it with as much vigour and pressure as you can stand. It was one of those big ones. This monster was well over an inch across and needed properly slaying. The experience is eye-wateringly painful, but the result is nothing short of miraculous. If done properly, one carefully applied Compeed artificial skin plaster can have you striding forward limp-free in less than 30 minutes.

Unfortunately, on this occasion "properly" is not what I did. In my haste I forgot perhaps the most important bit of blister preparation; my underlining of the word 'dried' in the last paragraph gives a clue. My notes tell me that I "forgot to dry heel" and as a result the newly applied Compeed

Galashiels Academy with SUW signpost (pic from 2005)

plaster, the only one I had of that brand, promptly "fell off". I had a.n.other branded plaster with which I made a second attempt; that stuck but it hurt like crazy and did not give the instant relief that I remembered from the WHW in 1999. I had no choice but to leave Hospital Bench, grit my teeth and continue climbing up and around the western flanks of Gala Hill, doing a quick graffiti check on Galashiels Academy and then on out into open country. My mistakes were to be costly in both time and money. I was also learning lessons about how unforgiving military-grade boots are.

Progress was slow. Although the pain in my heel was not severe it was only 'dulled' and became a definite discomfort and distraction on what was otherwise a superb section of the walk. The love affair with the River Tweed which was my watery companion of the last few miles of St Cuthbert's Way was not over. Once past the academy and the surrounding woodland the path gained modest height up to a handsome cairn at the unnamed col to the east of Hog Hill, and then quickly lost it again descending past Calfshaw Farmhouse to cross the River Tweed on the A707 at Fairnilee Farm. Having met the 'Three Brethren' before I immediately recognised the poise and

View towards Galashiels from cairn on the pass to the east of Hog Hill; woodland covers Gala Hill to the right

style of the cairn. It is much smaller than the famous three but seemed to be somehow preparing me for the close encounter to come.

On the whole the River Tweed is gorgeous from source to sea. It is particularly beautiful hereabouts but unfortunately the busy traffic-controlled Yair Bridge does not give much chance of a peaceful contemplative river encounter. It is nevertheless worth standing in one of the pedestrian refuges on the ancient bridge to admire the swirling waters and do a bit of 'big fish' spotting. I remembered to take a picture of the river, but totally forgot to take one of the bridge, which is why I have inserted another one here from my 2005 SUW walk. Unless something disastrous has happened, it will not have changed much.

Yair Bridge carries the A707 over the River Tweed

Once across the bridge a welcome right turn takes you away from the road and along the track at the bottom of Lindinny Wood. At last, the real star turn of the SUW commences in the company of the Shorthope Burn, passing Friars Croft, up Red Score Nick to emerge from the Yair Hill Forest just beyond the quaintly named 'Little Crib'. Yes, I just read the map again as I am having to do all the time to keep track of my memories. In reality I did not notice any of these features on this day, if indeed they were there to be noticed, but the names are excellent. Above the forest boundary the SUW turns north-west into a 'land of cairns' bringing the anticipated Three Brethren quickly into view. Walking the SUW in the usual westerly direction for many walkers they are more of an 'at last I thought I'd never get there' type encounter, heading east as I was doing it is more of a case of 'wow so soon already'.

Grinning and bearing it ~ moral support from one of the Three Brethren

Research tells me that The Three Brethren, perched at an altitude of 380 metres, date back to the 16th century. They were constructed by the lairds of Yair, Selkirk and Philiphaugh to mark the boundary of their respective estates. Each cairn is around nine feet high.

It was good to be reunited with these magnificent cairns. On the Southern Upland Way, the hilltop at the Three Brethren affords one of the best viewpoints, if not *the* best, along the whole of the 212-mile route. It was nearly 4pm by the time I arrived at the cairns; being only just past the halfway mark of today's walk. Tempting to rest my weary legs as it was, I could not hang around with the best part of 10 miles of mainly high-level moorland walking on the Old Drove Road to Traquair to do. I was properly grinning and bearing it, but the scenery was just so magnificent that somehow, thankfully, just for a few moments, it distracted me from the distraction at the end of my right leg.

Three Brethren plus brother trig ~ the Eildon Hills at the start of this day's walk can be seen in the distance

The Southern Upland Way follows the Old Drove Road over Broomy Law and Brown Knowe

My slow pace continued. Getting to Traquair from the Three Brethren was taking a lot longer than I recalled in the opposite direction nine years earlier. At that time, I think I was surprised how quickly I arrived in their company despite the rumours and reputation of an ever-receding goal similar to the southern ascent of Great Shunner Fell on the Pennine Way.

Beyond Brown Knowe you enter Traquair Forest still following the Old Drove Road. About a mile further on and feeling more determined than ever to keep going, something caught my attention; had aliens landed overnight? On the flanks of Minch Moor at Pipers Knowe something unusual had manifested in the heather. Strange circles filled my eyes. Was I hallucinating?

The 'Point of Resolution' sculpture

The plaque explains that the…

"'Point of Resolution' is a conservation project and a sculpture."

…and was completed in May 2005.

Looking through the 'Point of Resolution'

Looking back, I cannot recall seeing any evidence of this happening the last time I passed this spot on Friday the 6th of May 2005. All I can assume is that Charles Poulsen and his assistant Sam Wade who, the plaque suggests, carried out the heather cutting, were not far behind. As a quick look on Google Earth at map reference NT 354337 will confirm, the circles are in fact nowhere near circular but have been cut very carefully to appear as though they are, taking perspective and the lie of the land into account.

Again, quoting the plaque:

"The heather in the sculpture has been cut back to stimulate new growth, so providing a better food source for the grouse." and *"From the Resolution Point you will see a series of 'circles'. However, as you move away from the Resolution Point you will notice that they are not circles at all but huge irregular elongated ovals (the largest is 150 metres long and only 30 metres wide). The sculpture will keep changing with the seasons over many years."*

The plaque goes on to describe 'Point of Resolution' as:

"…a pilot project, which is intended to promote the idea of growing sculpture along the length of the Southern Upland Way (the 'Landworks' project) as a way of encouraging more people to use this most beautiful of routes."

Hear here I say, and what a fabulous ambition! Disappointing though that those mysterious rings have nothing to do with aliens.

I finally arrived at Quair View B&B in Traquair at 7.40pm. I was not in a good way when I arrived but landlady Pat who, amazingly, remembered me from nine years earlier, was an absolute angel. After showing me to my room she quickly got me sorted with poached eggs and tomatoes on toast, hot tea followed by a hot bath and a very welcome bed. That evening I made an emotional call to basecamp such were the physical pains of the previous few hours. Stopping made them worse; continuing the walk was in doubt. This was a typical day four of recent walks; each one preceding this had a similar hiatus.

People ask me if I train in some way ahead of a long walk. The answer is no I do not because there is little point. Apart from making sure I have got enough Compeed packed (memo to self) and other essentials in addition to good clothing, boots, socks, tent, sleepmat and bag basics, all you can do is prepare mentally. As far as the actual walking goes, I have learned that the only way

Quair View in 2014 ~ please note that B&B is no longer offered here (under new ownership)

to 'train' is to schedule the first few days very carefully, not over-stretching in terms of mileage or terrain. Those first few days are my training for the tougher and longer days ahead. I always try to plan my long walks this way; for me personally the only way is to get going and pace myself, although as demonstrated this can be easier said than done.

On this walk the early challenges that I was facing were all consequential of that failed, planned, fourth campsite in Divet Ha' Wood that meant walking all those additional miles on day three. Thirty-one miles so early on in this walk was nothing short of ridiculous. Looking back at my itinerary the outcome of all this was that three relatively simple day walks had become two tough ones. This combined with one wasted Compeed (how many mentions?!) at Hospital Bench led to the plight that I was now in. All this sounds a bit exaggerated and over-dramatic as I type these words in the comfort of home, but the world of a solo walker is a very small one indeed. There is you, the objective, and the experiences along the way. That's it.

I stayed at Quair View two days; I had little choice if I wanted to continue the walk.

It was rest or go home.

I chose rest.

TIME TO REST

Recuperation in Traquair

Rest Days ~ Going nowhere

Monday April 21 • Rest Day 1

This is not a book about going nowhere so I will keep my account of my rest days brief. I could just ignore them and move straight on to part 3 of this book but that would be a bit odd. Apart from the obvious gap in the dates it would be wrong to ignore what were really important days that put me back on that thin line west.

I slept well and woke up feeling simultaneously relieved that any walking would be optional but also frustrated at not being able to carry on. Rest days always make me feel this way; planned or not.

After breakfast, which I asked for to be as late as possible at 9am, I busied myself with more attention to my foot. I was meticulous in soaking, cleaning, drying, and giving my heel the best chance possible to at least start healing, so I could be confident that it would heal completely in the quickest time possible.

Apparently, I had some additional Compeed plasters, but I cannot for the life of me remember where they came from. Had I lost them in my rucksack; did I get more when Pat took me to Innerleithen; did Pat just give me some out of her own supplies? I have no idea. There is nothing telling in my notes, but I am sure I went into town; that was to get a memorable Indian takeaway that was way more than I could manage at one sitting. Anyway, whatever transpired, I had more of those precious plasters! Hereafter I am going to make a serious effort not to mention them any more in this book (notice I said *this* book).

Traquair

The rest of the day was exceedingly lazy. I passed time updating social media, drying out gear, looking at maps, reading tourist leaflets and watching daytime television. Outside the weather was once again gorgeous, but I was enjoying doing as little as possible. This was a day when I really did not care why what or when. I dislike the expression 'me time' but admittedly that is exactly what it was, although it could be argued that all of my walks are exercises in self-indulgence!

Tuesday April 22 • Rest Day 2

Referring again to my itinerary I am reminded that I had in fact planned yesterday as a rest day. This was because of previous day four experiences on Offa's Dyke and the Southern Upland Way. However, two rest days was not in the plan, but as explained earlier, completely necessary. You can tell by the way I am writing here that I do get strange and totally unnecessary feelings of guilt about rest days. Where do they come from? I was after all supposed to be on holiday enjoying myself!

Today I had it in mind to go into Peebles to stock up on food supplies but then Pat's husband Brian offered to give me an early morning lift into Innerleithen again, where I got everything that I needed. Going into Peebles did not feel right anyway, especially on wheels, as that was the next town on the walking route. I walked the 1½ miles back to Traquair, hobbling a bit but not too bad. It was good to check that my foot care was yielding results, which it was. I felt confident about donning boots and rucksack and leaving in the morning.

Also, part of the plan was to send a change of clothes to Quair View; this Janine had done just after I left Macclesfield; the usual shoe box had been waiting for me on arrival. With hindsight it seems a bit early for all of this, but I was glad to box up the stuff I had worn over the last week and send it back home and to get into fresh clothes. Additional clean socks were particularly welcome; the ones I had worn over the last few days could have found their own way south. I also sent home the usual random collection of stuff that seems oh so important to take but in reality, is never really needed. It happens every time. One of these days I will take what I actually *need* and nothing more!

The afternoon was spent doing yet more footcare. During the evening I spent a couple of hours doing a rucksack review on Facebook, the first time I had reviewed anything on social media. It helped pass some time getting into the minutiae of my Lightwave 'Wildtrek 70'. I think it got half-a-dozen likes. Well, I thought it was useful even if no-one else did.

Here I would like to make special mention of my hosts at Quair View B&B, Patricia Hudson, and her now late husband Brian. They were just so kind and did all they could to help me to get going again.

Breakfast at Quair View and a custom Ordnance Survey map 😊

Being directly on the Southern Upland Way they doubtless saw a lot of walkers but whatever the case I felt I received hospitality fit for a VIP. It was two days when I felt very much at home. My sincere thanks to both of them. Suffice to say the breakfasts at Quair View were excellent. Rocket fuel for the days to come!

I was going to need it…

PART THREE

Cross Borders Droving

Traquair to East Calder

Wednesday April 23, day 5 ● Traquair to Romanno Bridge

Tweed Bridge

Feeling the benefit of two rest days and after another fabulous early breakfast at Quair View I bade farewell to my hosts and got going. An overcast grey-skied day five immediately presented a choice of routes to restart the walk. My original intention was to continue following the Cross Borders Drove Road west from Traquair over the substantial range of hills topped by Kirkhope Law, but not wanting to overdo it and undo my recuperation I decided a gentle riverside walk would be the best way of getting back into my stride, hopefully without waking the beast under my right heel. Once again, the magic attractions of the River Tweed were at work. There is something inherently soothing about being alongside a substantial river, so I went out onto the road at Quair View and turned right towards Innerleithen and descended to the riverside at Tweed Bridge before entering the town. I would re-join the Cross Borders Drove Road in Peebles.

Route planning in Scotland is harder than it is in England. Not due to a shortage of paths but because all the helpful green or red broken lines on Ordnance Survey (OS) maps stop at the border reflecting the difference in respective jurisdictions with regard to access rights in Scotland and Rights of Way in England. Discerning exactly where footpaths are can sometimes be difficult. So far on the route, apart from two short sections either side of the Eildon Hills, I had been following waymarked long distance paths in the shape of the St Cuthbert's Way and the Southern Upland Way. Thankfully, these *are* marked on OS maps with green or red diamonds and as a result you can be reasonably confident that the routes are 1) accessible, 2) open and 3) on the whole well-defined. Beyond those recognised trails further help is needed…

Without doubt the most helpful and authoritative source of information for walkers in Scotland is the

Scottish Rights of Way and Access Society (also known as Scotways). Founded in 1845 Scotways is an independent charity which upholds and promotes public access rights in Scotland. Their book 'Scottish Hill Tracks' is invaluable for finding routes in the absence of them being marked on OS mapping. Highly recommended. More information at scotways.com.

Cardrona pedestrian bridge (detail shown below)

The walk to Peebles was pleasant enough and for the most part easy, but you could never quite escape the noise of the traffic on the nearby A72 road. At Cardrona walkers are encouraged across a modern suspension bridge built for cyclists and pedestrians only. It is a good example of modern architecture fitting into the landscape and riverside environment well. OS maps suggest that a pathway squeezes between road and river hereabouts, but my guess is you would end up road walking, the former being built so tightly up to the latter.

River Tweed and the A72 from Cardrona pedestrian bridge

Not far beyond the bridge I suddenly found myself surrounded by what looked like a very recently built housing estate, full of properties all built pretty much at the same time, and all desperately trying to look different from one another but somehow failing; some with red clay tile roofs others with grey artificial slate roofs, some walled with brick, others stone and some rendered. At the time I walked through all looked neat and pleasant enough but odd at the same time. The mix of roof

Cardrona

styles was nothing short of baffling; it was if an entire architectural school of students had been let loose with their own interpretations of the best ways of achieving 'faux'. Sorry people of Cardrona I am not being very complimentary about your estate; so long as you are happy there then that is all that matters. It must be good to live so near the river, I just hope your houses are built above the flood plain, it looks like a close call to me.

Having walked through the housing estate and with my mind awash with architectural observations, I crossed back over the Tweed on a bridge; trouble is I cannot remember which one! According to the map I should have used the old railway bridge, but for reasons unknown I am as sure as I can be that I missed it and ended up crossing the road bridge that links the now formerly named Cardrona Village with the A72. Whatever the truth of the matter I ended up walking across my least favourite of all places: a golf course. This will be a subject I will return to at some point either in this book or others; suffice to say right here right now that I dislike them (stronger language is in mind).

Beyond the golf course things went rapidly downhill. The generous well-surfaced path for pedestrians and cyclists that starts life on the old railway bridge became a track which became a narrowing and uncertain path, which on the face of it was okay, but it got a bit unnerving when I found myself wandering between the rear of the Eshiels Community Recycling Centre and the local sewage works. I did not have to break through fences, climb gates or any other dubious activity, the pathway through kept going, but it still had a distinct air of uncertainty about it.

Having made enquiries locally during the rest days I had been informed of a 'pleasant riverside walk' from Innerleithen to Peebles. All I can assume is that it was a work in progress. Is it complete today in 2021 I wonder? If it is they have done something very clever a 100 yards or so beyond the last pair of circular gravel washes at the sewage works, because the path abruptly stopped at a cottage garden that sloped all the way down to the river some way below. There was a strong whiff of shall we call it 'local intervention' about it. Thick aggressive brambles, a red 'No entry' sign and a set of new wooden steps heading up to the busy road apparently without an exit onto it told its own story. I went up and escaped onto the road feeling annoyed and in danger. I was wishing that I had turned left out of Quair View to take the Cross

Once upon a time there was a path?

Borders Drove Road over the hills. With hindsight it would have been easier, troublesome right foot included.

Thankfully, I was not on the road for long happily regaining access back down to the riverside just beyond the cottage driveway. From there, at last, things improved, and a very pleasant riverside walk followed direct into Peebles town centre.

At the riverside I got into conversation with a cyclist and shared common interests and generally enjoyed 20 minutes of pass-the-time-of-day chit-chat. Nice fella. Walkers and cyclists can sometimes have a 'strained' relationship, but on this occasion, there was not even a hint of tension.

I really should not stereotype, nasty habit, although there is a particular type of what some have termed 'militant' cyclist that I have had the odd unfortunate encounter with. You will have to read about my 2019 walk for more on that subject. Let me leave it there, this is supposed to be an account of a peaceful idyllic walk in the hills; time to move on…

Approaching Peebles

With blue skies reappearing, albeit it temporarily, I was keen to get back among the hills although my notes tell me that I stopped for a pint in Peebles. Unfortunately, they do not reveal where, or how good the beer was or what it was. All very remiss of me, but when I did eventually get on my way, on my right I passed what I assumed from a distance to be the town hall (and now discover is in fact the local parish church) followed by some fine stone terraced houses on Young Street. Continuing out of town I headed for the forested slopes of Crailzie Hill and my target for the day at Romanno Bridge. A lingering acquaintance with the evidently attractive riverside town of Peebles would have to wait.

Looking back towards Peebles from the lane on Hamilton Hill

For now, at last, I had to tear myself away from the River Tweed. It was time for the river to lose its grip and release me to go north. A few miles west of Peebles the Tweed turns east having already flowed a

considerable distance from its source to the north of Moffat and therefore away from my direction of travel. It was time to part company with one of my favourite waterways; present on my shortlist because it finds the sea at one of my favourite seaside towns; Spittal. Have I surprised you? Maybe you thought I was going to mention the place across the river that takes its name? I love Berwick-upon-Tweed as well of course, I just prefer Spittal; despite its name being somewhat less endearing.

Infant trees line the path near Courhope

It was good to be back on the hills again and this time I had the first substantial bit of forest to look forward to. The Southern Upland Way is sometimes criticised for its lack of variety and in particular for many long sections of walking in what some other commentator's words describe as 'dark depressing timber factories'. I did not find it that way; if anything, it gave me an appreciation not so much of 'dark and depressing' but more often much needed shelter with a bonus hit on other senses such as smell; I love the smell of trees! Forests can be gloomy of that there is no doubt, but I love the feeling of security they give. Some people find them claustrophobic, even threatening being historically perceived as places of danger, but I like them, and I don't stop liking them when they're being worked and felled; particularly when properly managed as most of them are these days. On a warm sunny day, you can get almost dizzy with the heavy heady sappy aroma as you walk beside huge timber stacks. Memories of 2005 and the Southern Upland Way came flooding back.

Recollections of the Southern Upland Way became particularly focussed not many yards into the forest near Courhope where a number of trees were blocking my path. Getting past was more challenging than you might expect with drainage ditches on one side and dense forest on the other with three fallen trees filling the gap between. Get past I did but not without a fight and getting various bits of shock-cord caught on the way through, which at one point effectively flung me back to where I just started. Vicious!

Once beyond the forest a pleasant walk on springy green turfed tracks between hills followed; good therapy for any easily disturbed 'creatures' that may be residing under your right heel. So far so good today; whilst I was not totally 'out of the woods' (forgive me) at least I was walking normally and with reasonable pace nearly maxing out at 3mph! Life was good and I was at last starting to feel as though I had a fighting chance of getting to Iona, although on this night reality would hit home a bit with a return to the tent. No more B&B luxury for now, although it was to be the last night in a tent until on the West Highland Way; the next three nights once more to be in a proper bed. Cheating? Maybe so in the opinion

Cross Borders Drove Road at Fingland Burn between Drum Maw (rising to the left) and Hag Law (right)

of some but I am here to enjoy myself, not indulge in discomfort. I get the tent out when I need it; until then it stays on my back to help keep me grounded. Do I hear 'be prepared'? Good idea.

I saw no-one all the way from Peebles to Romanno Bridge. Except for sheep and tadpoles. Yes tadpoles! Quite how these little aquatic marvels get 300 metres up on a shepherd's track is well, to say the least, determined, on the part of these tiny amphibians that must have climbed up from the burn. See what I did there - I did not commit to frog or toad. I will guess frog. Far be it from me to commit to paper my scant knowledge of all things herpetological. Yes, I did look that up.

Wildlife studies on 'Herpetology Hill'

With the Pentland Hills now coming into view the good walking continued down to Romanno Bridge where I had arranged one of my more unusual places to camp. I was given permission to pitch my tent in the grounds of the Newlands Centre which, as the proudly polished brass plaque declared, had been opened two years earlier by a VIP. What was originally a village primary school had now expanded to become a multi-purpose activity centre (online at newlandscentre.org.uk).

My original plan was to wild camp somewhere in the vicinity of grid reference NT 182476 (for those that like a bit of detail) but during my recuperation break in Traquair I found Newlands with its irresistible over-fifty friendly 'facilities'. Having seen the place that I had planned to camp, which again referring to my notes was "marshy/reedy" (and probably midgy), I was very pleased that I camped as suggested. I met the caretaker who showed me the facilities I had access to which were all excellent and still smelled of polish, new paint, and rubber. All very satisfactory although I did have to be off site by 8am the next morning…

Camp 5 in the company of the polytunnels at Newlands

Thursday was after all an ordinary school day. Public relations are not helped by parents and children seeing some random camper wandering around his tent early doors. Such an event might have aroused more curiosity and interest than I would have welcomed and was therefore best avoided. Various evening classes were taking place the night I stayed until about 10pm so I could access all the facilities I needed at my leisure. Knowing that early next morning I would pass the 100-mile marker since leaving Lindisfarne, despite slow progress and an unscheduled rest day, I was content to be where I was, and, as a result, I slept well on one of the comfiest patches of grass you could hope for. For now, all was well.

Remarkably, Ordnance Survey celebrate this personal detail on their maps by indicating a farmhouse called 'Paulswell', presumably so named after the adjacent 'Paul's Well', a short mile north of Romanno Bridge. How very generous of them but not worth the fifty quid it would have cost me to include a teeny extract from their Landranger sheet number 65 here. Factcheck this for yourself if you should so wish!

Whilst talking about placenames and if per chance you have reached for your map, you may also have noticed the discrepancy between the way Ordnance Survey indicates 'Romannobridge' and the way I am presenting the name of the village in this book. Both forms of the name are used by the OS and Wikipedia, the former referring to the physical bridge carrying the A701 road over Lyne Water as

Romanno Bridge, the latter likewise referencing both. The Newlands Centre address supports the two-word version so I shall defer to local knowledge and precedent. Placenames can be very sensitive things!

Thursday April 24, day 6 ● Romanno Bridge to East Calder

Awake at 5.30am and despite ongoing blister niggles I was looking forward to crossing the Pentland Hills. Somehow it was a name, in this case and in my mind of an obscure range of hills, that I had always been aware of even though at this point I had never set foot on them. I remember a similar awareness of the Howgill Fells, for years seeing them when rushing by on the M6 but never doing anything about my hopeless lack of adventure on them, until that is I noticed that they had come to the attention of Wainwright. That was a call to action…

Tent life

I recall a memorable mid-eighties day on the Howgills with a work colleague, another Paul, climbing up to The Calf from the Lune Valley at Howgill, close by the M6 and the West Coast Main Line. It was memorable not just because the Howgills are among the least known, unspoilt, and most beautiful hills in England, but also because two Pauls got totally lost. Well not so much lost as disorientated. I remember our 'concern' on our descent as we gazed down into the valley before us; both the motorway and the railway line were 'missing'. Yes, we were looking at the Lune Valley again but sadly for us, late in the day, we were gazing north not west. Clearly, I had not heeded Wainwright's advice, given on page 5 of his introduction to the Howgill Fells, in his book 'Walks on the Howgill Fells', about navigation challenges when leaving The Calf.

Back to 2014: As I woke I was relieved to discover that my tent was not frozen stiff. Apart from a bit of condensation on the inside it was quite dry, which was good news because that meant a lighter rucksack.

The day started with an uneventful minor road walk into West Linton where I was able to stock up with nibbles for the day. One mile out of the village you are back amongst the hills skirting the western end of Mount Maw at Faw Mount on the Cross Borders Drove Road soon also to become the 'Thieves Road'. Place names rooted in history are always of interest to me, but they can get confused and intertwined. The intrigue did not stop when I realised that my next objective was

The Pentland Hills from the road to West Linton

'Cauldstane Slap' which marks the watershed of the Pentland Hills. I seem to remember getting into deep conversation with the locals about this most curious of names, although little information and enlightenment was forthcoming from these big brown hairy-horned beasties. I am going to have to look this one up before commenting further.

Highland cattle are just the most delightful of creatures. One is well aware that with a single well-aimed swoop of that noble head they could inflict serious and life-threatening trauma, but unlike yaks of

Himalayan fame you feel absolutely no sense of danger in their company. Maybe I am too relaxed about their presence, others might feel different! They are just beautiful; the peace-loving hippies of the Highlands who I relate to so very well indeed. Whenever I see them, I get an almost irresistible desire to sit down amongst the grass and heather with them and offload all my problems. I have not done it yet, but I am sure that instant karma and perhaps a slight whiff of farmyard would result; maybe accompanied by the odd excitable winged insect taking up residence about my person. Today they just kept a watchful but unconcerned eye on me as I passed by, closer communion would have to wait.

This is fine walking country, and no wonder why it is so very popular with the residents of Edinburgh and surrounding areas less than 10 miles away. Apart from any delays suffered by chatting to disinterested bovines, progress seemed quick on the northbound ascent from Baddinsgill Reservoir to Cauldstane Slap. At a relaxed pace I made good time and arrived there at 10.40am two hours after leaving West Linton. Clearly my hairy hippy friends were a very good distraction from my foot problems.

Dark clouds brooding over Cauldstane Slap and East Cairn Hill (looking north)

Now, Cauldstane Slap. What is it exactly? My 2021 research takes me once again to Wikipedia, but on this occasion, horror of horrors, despite an entry being found there, it is of no use. Neither are, somewhat surprisingly, the information signs hereabouts. Plenty of useful words about the history of the place and its use, but nothing forthcoming about the meaning of the names. Further searching reveals the next paragraph, quoting from the Heritage Paths' website at heritagepaths.co.uk:

"A 'slap' is a pass, the root of which can be seen in the Slug Road in Aberdeenshire and the Slochd on the A9 south of Inverness. Cauldstane probably refers to the wind that can whip over the pass and when walked it feels like a very remote and quiet place."

There, now we know. A slap is a pass. Easy! And we have an idea of the meaning of Cauldstane; game set and match I would say. Aren't you glad I have brought all of this together for you?

Suffice to say I knew none of this as I dumped my rucksack at the watershed fence to take five and admire the view to the north-west. Was that my first glimpse of the distant Highlands? Pulse raced, I reckoned it was, although I did not hang around for long. Great as the view was, I was itching for the next stage of the walk, but with some miles to go to my planned overnight non-tent stopover in East Calder, it was time to leave the southern uplands behind and descend with the Thieves and Drovers down to Little Vantage and another couple of miles of road walking. So far, the weather on this day had been overcast with threatening looking clouds but almost as if by magic, as soon as I started the descent, blue skies changed the whole mood and feel of the walk. With well over 100 miles behind me I suddenly felt that I was making real progress!

In contrast to the south-eastern approach to the Pentlands which with attractive hills all around seem to pass by quickly, the north-western descent is immediate and across open moorland. The distance from the watershed to the road is half that from the road in West Linton but it seems to take a lot longer; all an illusion I suppose; I guess I must have been giddy with anticipation of what was to come. The Pentland Hills were though a lot broader than I expected them to be. It is strange how an impression gained from years of looking at maps can deeply ingrain your idea of what a place might be like. Of course, the distances we

The view north-west from Cauldstane Slap with Harperrig Reservoir in the middle distance

are talking about here are on a very modest scale even by Scottish standards but that is how these hills seemed to me on this day in April 2014. Another place I need to revisit.

Long-distance walkers might be regarded as people who know their country well, but in reality, we only ever really make passing acquaintance with the places we walk through. If anything, the experience of travelling on foot opens your eyes to just how little we know of the country we call home. This is all part of the 'sizing up' experience and is to be expected. Getting to grips with distance is, as the name suggests, what long-distance walkers do best. However, on the way you find yourself building an ever increasing list of places that you feel obliged to revisit. There is of course no obligation, but be assured, forever afterwards you are wanting, even yearning, to return to that town, that village, that pub; those hills.

If you ever feel the need to make your roots in your homeland go deeper, if you can and if you are blessed with time and ability, get your boots on, and walk. I can think of no better way.

The Pentland Hills quickly recede from the view as you approach the road at Little Vantage

The car park at Little Vantage lies hidden amongst the trees

I love the way that the sign (seen in these pictures) at Little Vantage car park on the A70 directs the walker to 'The' Cauldstane Slap. It gives the impression that either punishment or a strange new dance on top of the Pentland Hills are imminent!

I reached the end of the Cross Borders Drove Road, also known as the Thieves Road, feeling accomplished. From this point forward I was on a new and significant stage of the walk. Lands of canals, engineering and urban environs were ahead. All felt very safe and rural again. No more two-horned hairy monsters, no more slapping or other indecent punishments, no more threatening dark clouds. I always enjoy the contrast between the wild and the not-so-wild. Somehow it always feels good to leave the one and enter the other. The grass is always greener on the other side, so they say.

The weather was bright and breezy as I turned right onto the road edge and walked with increased pace along the wide grass verge. With Arthur's Seat in the middle of Edinburgh clearly in view, the feeling of progress expressed earlier was further reinforced. For just under two miles the main A70 road was mercifully traffic-free, but nonetheless I was glad to leave it and turn left down Leyden Road (a country lane) towards the day's objective.

Walking north on the A70 with Arthur's Seat clearly in view (centre of picture)

At precisely two-o'clock, after calling in at the Post Office and sending used maps home, I was in The Grapes on East Calder's Main Street with a pint of beer and the now obligatory fish n chips on the table in front of me. The food was fantastic, genuinely it was, as was the pint of Belhaven bitter, although I have been known to go overboard with culinary praise after a full day's walk. For me these are the things that tell me that I am in Scotland proper: passing place signs, highland cattle, and a pint of beer from the country's oldest brewery. There was no turning back now, once again I am hooked by Scotland's allure with the best still to come.

Content as I was sat solo in the lounge bar of this fine public house on a Thursday mid-afternoon, I was suddenly struck with a feeling of unease. Had I walked too quickly? Was I (dread to think now) rushing this walk and trying to make up for lost time at Traquair? Ah yes, all this was yet another signal of transition from daily life into the slower life that is involved when backpacking and walking a long way. It takes me usually about a week before I settle into the rhythm of new circumstances that a long-distance walk always brings. I had forgotten that my days were starting early, especially when in the tent; I was after all up at 5.30am. Stop panicking man! Sit there, eat food, thank God for the here and now and drink your beer!

I think I might have I listened to myself...

My accommodation for my one night in East Calder had been pre-arranged by a friend from my local church in Macclesfield. I was to stay at the home of Marion and Bill Thompson only a few minutes' walk away from the pub. I was in a sorry state when I arrived, well I probably looked that way. Once again, the roaring fire under my right heel had ignited and I was limping badly. It was really odd because throughout the day's walk across the Pentlands I hardly felt it at all, in fact on the descent from Cauldstane Slap I had totally forgotten about it. The road walking was the cause although stopping for an hour in The Grapes did not help. I had only done a few miles of on the roadside from Little Vantage, but it was enough. My feet in this particular pair of military boots were just not happy partners, but I was determined to adapt to them and get used to them. I knew they were good boots; my feet were always dry; it was just a fact that the soles and particularly the heels were in no way resilient being hard solid rubber. They were after all designed for military service, not for my pussy-feet on big hills in Scotland.

Marion put her laundry facilities at my disposal. I took advantage of her rotary washing line and floated the tent over it to air it out and hopefully get it dry before it rained, the skies having morphed from blue to grey. The few clothes I had were also washed and dried. You see, right there, a reason why pyjamas are necessary. I have learned the lessons of minimal clothing; I really am able to make do with one decent set of essentials and counted in that list are spare socks and PJs. They are light and really useful, not just

Bill and Marion's welcoming front door

for making yourself feel comfortable in the alien grip of a sleeping bag, but for situations like this where the alternative would be oh so much worse.

Dressed once again in clean clothes I joined Marion, Bill and family for a very agreeable tea including a superb Lasagne for main course which sat really contentedly on top of the fish n chips I had consumed in The Grapes only a few hours earlier. Conversation ebbed and flowed; the company being really welcome. After tea Marion gifted me a modest bottle whisky. My notes tell me I was given it "…for my laryngitis." Honest! Needless to say, I slept well.

This is the only overnight accommodation for which I do not have a photo record. I forgot to take one but on request Bill kindly provided the pic seen here.

PART FOUR

Canal Land

East Calder to Kirkintilloch

Friday April 25, day 7 ● East Calder to Polmont

Almondell & Calderwood Country Park

River Almond

Equine watchers

My day started with a heart and heels prayer. The former because my ongoing arrythmia problem was being a pest and the latter for reasons that by this stage of my walking recollections you know well enough. I was not in a particular state of panic, more one of "I wish these things would just do one and stop spoiling my day!"

Once outside again I was fine and with a quick route revision I decided to start the day with a walk through the local park rather than roads to get to the canal; and what a park it was. Almondell & Calderwood Country Park is a thin ribbon of woodland glory strung along the River Almond just to the north of East Calder; and was exactly the launch I needed into a few days that were to feature a lot of water.

I do not know what people in the East Calder locality think to their park, but I thought it was a gem. It had an air of maturity, even a dash of wildness about it which, for an essentially urban park with the Calders to the south, Livingston to the west, Broxburn to the north and the M8 motorway in-between, I thought was quite stunning. These places are just so precious, particularly in locations where open space within reach of a big city is at a premium.

Sadly, the parkland encounter did not last for long. Within a few minutes of leaving by the north entrance I was passing under the M8 motorway, but spirit was once again lifted; this time by the strangest of means: some sort of holy graffiti! That is an assumption on my part of course, but this was not the first time that I have encountered well placed seemingly totally coincidental 'words of encouragement'.

Maybe subconsciously someone was plugging into feelings of apprehension I sometimes experience when passing through unknown 'urban wilds' that I occasionally encounter on these walks. As expressed before

'Holy graffiti' under the M8 motorway

I enjoy these encounters, but I do get built-up area butterflies, which I suppose are there to keep me on my guard for the unexpected. Most people are friendly and welcoming, but I have had a few encounters that have rocked me out of my solo solace into a place that I hate being, one of confrontation, albeit usually minor in nature. I must emphasise though that this has not always been with humans; dogs in particular can cause feelings more like bats than butterflies. Anyway whatever the reason for the "Be Not Afraid" graffiti, I was pleased to see it and took it on board at face value. So thank you to whoever wielded the aerosol but please don't do it again, some might think it holy, others might regard it as vandalism!

With gorgeous country park, horses and three strategically located words to calm the soul under a comforting and all too familiar 'Macclesfield grey' sky, and with a bounce in my step, I descended down from the road to join my watery companions for the next two days; the Union, Forth and Clyde Canals.

A grey day on the Union Canal south of Broxburn

It felt great to be on the canal towpath. Not only because I knew it guaranteed safe and hopefully unobstructed passage all the way to Kirkintilloch, and most of it on a level and well-maintained path, but also because of its familiarity. My hometown of Macclesfield often languishes under a leaden-grey sky that can hang heavy for days on end, but it is a proud town, thanks in a lesser sense to the authorities and in a greater sense to Maxonians who are on the whole friendly, stoic, down-to-earth let's-get-on-with-life type people. I have grown to love Macclesfield (known locally as Macc and pronounced by true Maxonians 'Makkersfield') since 'emigrating' there from Stockport in 1995. Yes it is that different…

Macclesfield is a canal town that gives its name to one of the most scenic canals on the entire UK network. Canal walks for me, Janine, and our two black Boradors Max and Meggy, are a part of everyday life (Boradors are a Border Collie + Labrador crossbreed). Resulting from these daily encounters, owning a share in a narrowboat for a time, my involvement for a few years in the Canal and River Trust's Historic Working Boats Group, plus being descended from Truswells of old that worked on the canals (now morphed into Truswell Haulage), you could say that canals are in my blood; without water borne diseases of the Weils variety you understand. I feel a deep kinship and affinity with them.

That reminds me; having mentioned our dogs can I clear something up (forgive the pun). With regard to my long solo walks I get asked "why don't you take the dogs for company?" or words to that effect. There are a few words that come to mind in defence of my abject refusal to do this; words like 'stile' for example or 'cows' or 'sheep'. Those just for starters. There is also the teeny consideration of destination and my desire to actually arrive there. Taking Max and Meggy would seriously compromise the likelihood of my achieving this. You see they want to play, a lot. They don't give a tuppenny hoot about me and my walking ambitions. Then there's the food, the sleeping accommodation whether in my tent or elsewhere, poo 'management', and their desire to socialise noisily and defend me from pretty much anything that moves. By the way, they would insist on being in the tent and then try and eject me from my sleeping bag.

I love our two mad dogs dearly but no: no way! Moving swiftly on…

The Union Canal immediately played a trick on me. Very soon after joining it near Broxburn, once in the town the canal decides to ignore my desire to go west and instead heads east for a mile and a half. Granted the challenge to my sense of orientation did not last long but heading away from your objective always unnerves the long distance walker. Maybe dogs are not the only problem!

Let me not beat about the bush or wade in the shallows here… The Union Canal and particularly the Forth and Clyde Canal beyond it have some very long sections of monotonous walking. There are stretches of wooded beauty, moments of fascination and even some awesome engineering along the way as we shall see, but for the most part this is 'head up, face forward, quick march' territory, hence my pre-planning of three 17+ mile days on the trot. Canals are about progress and work; they were not built to entertain. Workers on the Macclesfield Canal were lucky having expansive views across Cheshire for much of their way along the cut, but it was engineering and commercial demand that made the navvies follow the contour of the hills above the plain, not the need for a nice view. I imagine families living on

The Union Canal north of Broxburn

Three-tier bridging ~ canal, road and the
Pardovan Burn intersect near Philpstoun

the waterways thereafter would have very little time in a working day to look at the view anyway; if they could see it that is, on many occasions the view would have been obscured by heavy acrid polluted air. Life was tough on the cut.

To the north-east of Broxburn at Winchburgh I was as close as I would get to the Firth of Forth and the bridges spanning across it at Queensferry just over two miles away, although I did not know that at the time. Even this early in spring the heavily wooded confines of the canal were denying any chance of a view. If there was one I missed it!

I was walking at a steady three miles per hour, which all these years later in 2021 as I tap away at this keyboard is really useful. Yes this is a book of recollections but in many cases recalling exactly where a picture was taken and what the subject matter was at the time can be challenging and time-consuming. However, with the steady pace I was progressing at on this particular day and armed with the Ordnance Survey's marvellous online mapping on my desktop, estimating my position on the ground based on the time stamps on the digital images works surprisingly well; the adjacent picture being a prime example.

Linlithgow Canal Centre from Manse Road

On my approach to Linlithgow I was diverted away from the towpath onto adjacent roads due to dredging works. Quite why that necessitated a closure of the towpath puzzled me, but there you go; don't ask. This was the busiest urban area I had encountered since leaving Galashiels and Melrose and came as quite a jolt to the senses, particularly after the peace and quiet of the towpath, although from my point of view it was a pleasant jolt.

From the elevated canal towpath in Linlithgow a pleasant jumble of historic buildings can be seen to the north, all seemingly piled up on one another looking very sturdy and satisfactory. Sadly, as a quick dive into Google StreetView will reveal, all is not well in this part of town from an architectural sensitivity standpoint. Quite what the local planning authorities were thinking when they allowed the construction of the concrete monstrosities on the High Street which overlook Kirkgate (the splendid approach to Linlithgow Palace), and The Cross Well is beyond me. Somebody seriously lost the plot here; and there's me thinking that the Market Place in Macclesfield had the worst example of historic town square despoilment. I wonder what they knocked down! Just appalling.

Seen from the canal front to back: Linlithgow Burgh Halls,
St Michael's Parish Church and Linlithgow Palace

The day continued overcast and grey, but the walking conditions were ideal; temperature about 14 degrees and dry with a slight breeze so I was motoring along and looking forward to one night in a Premier Inn: at least one night in a motel is an indulgence I insist on as part of my long walk itineraries. Corporate duvet predictability and connectivity, in contrast to most other nights on route which are marked by unpredictability and wildly varying degrees of comfort (or lack thereof), for just one night is a luxury that I always look forward to. Having said all this, motels rarely coincide with my routes as they favour locations near to major highways, which I tend to steer away from not gravitate towards, so it usually is for one night only.

Just over a mile west of Linlithgow you encounter the first of three engineering marvels on the Union Canal, the Avon Aqueduct, carrying as the name suggests, the canal over the River Avon. Tomorrow's walk will encounter both the Falkirk Canal Tunnel and the Falkirk Wheel. Canals are engineering marvels in their own way, but these types of structures are the star players deserving of admiration.

Designed by Hugh Baird (apparently with advice from Thomas Telford – well why wouldn't you?) the

Perspectives on the Avon Aqueduct and a view down to the river below

Avon Aqueduct was built between 1819 and 1821. At just over 810ft long and 86ft high above the river the aqueduct is carried on 12 stone arches each with a span of 50ft. It is a wonder to behold.

Another engineering marvel although not on my current list of three and not on the canal is the Grangemouth Oil Refinery. Not a thing of beauty, of that there is no doubt, but nonetheless it does draw attention to itself. As I approached Polmont the refinery is only a mile or so away, but it seemed more distant; it must have been a trick of the hazy light surrounding it. I suppose some might say that

Grangemouth Oil Refinery

the refinery is anything but marvellous, but my response to that is we would not have got so far in terms of transport and industrial development without places such as this. Indeed I would not be on this walk if it were not for places like this, because in daily life I would do nothing other than walk or ride a horse maybe; so why walk for recreation? Like it or not these places have driven progress, yes and polluted a lot along the way, but wait a minute here; who are the main polluters? Did we not demand the products of Grangemouth?

One day all this will change. Earlier this year (April 2021) I had my first ride in an all-electric car. Transport in the future is going to change radically but will it really be less polluting and have less impact on the environment as we gather the elements needed to build that mountain of batteries? We will see.

All this is going through my head as I walk. It is a good example of what can occupy my mind as I stroll along. Isn't it strange; I walk in part to escape, and then I find my subconscious wrapping itself with the world's concerns. Not a bad thing I guess. Once in the Highlands thoughts will rest on more relaxing themes.

In Polmont I left the canal at Station Road and walked north to find the promised land of a Premier Inn. My first thought was to see if I could get a bus or maybe a taxi to save my legs on the urban footpaths,

or, more specifically, I should say to ensure that the sleeping beast under my right heel was not once again woken from its apparent slumber. One of my unwritten 'rules' is that I do permit myself transport other than walking to or from off route overnight accommodation. On this occasion wheeled transport was not found and in the event was not needed because I happily discovered yet another pleasant urban park to walk through. The Gray Buchanan Park could not have been better located. Beyond the park I soon found myself on an easy road walk to my motel for the night on the A9 close to its junction with the M9 motorway. In my head the Premier Inn was a lot further from the canal, in reality it was a little over a mile and a half. At last, hopefully, I was past the pain of walking, it was now my transport of choice, even when off route.

At 3pm after some 18½ miles of generally easy walking, and without any noticeable discomfort emanating from my boots, I checked into the Premier Inn and started occupying the room, or should I say integrating with it. It was time to empty the rucksack entirely, check the state of its contents and let everything breathe as I ran an exceedingly deep and luscious bath fortified with every small bottle of shower gel, soap, or bubble bath I could find in the room. I dived in hoping to surface again an hour or so later. Do not disturb!

I sought food in the adjacent Brewers Fayre 'Cadgers Brae' refreshment establishment (note my reluctance to use the words 'restaurant' or 'pub') and ate my fill of unexceptional food. I savoured every mouthful. I am usually very fussy about pubs; when at home I seek out real pubs, not a restaurant with a bar attached. When I am walking it is a very different story; it is not that all of a sudden anything goes, let us just say I am more 'tolerant'. As long as I can get my standard order (come on you should know what that is by now) I am a very happy bunny indeed.

Top Gear and a full-on slob-out on the bed followed. I was contentment incarnate.

Tomorrow was another day.

Saturday April 26, day 8 ● Polmont to Kirkintilloch

I slept like a brick. Or was it a log. Until 5.45am. My body clock was now firmly entrenched in the daily walking routine. As I said earlier, it usually takes a week for me to settle into the rhythm.

Back in the Cadger's Brae I ate the biggest breakfast I could manage which on reflection was not that big; not because it was not available but because my appetite first thing in the morning, especially when walking, is not that great. You would think that this was the best opportunity possible to demonstrate the 'most important meal of the day' principle that, in the view of many, breakfast has always been. For me however, whilst I believe this to be true, it always feels too early, whether at 7am as in this case or later towards nine. I am an elevenses man, although I am not talking here about a brew (mash if east of the Pennines) but more about when hunger strikes. For me it does not happen on que, breakfast time often feels too early, lunchtime too late; an en-route mid-morning café at about 11am works perfectly.

Invoking my wheels allowed rule I called for a taxi at 7.45am back to the canal which duly turned up at the appointed time and dropped me off at Polmont railway station. Before dropping back down to the towpath it was time to get the supplies in, and on the way found a suitable shop which thankfully was open. This was not your typical eight-til-late shop, this was a proper family grocer, a rare thing indeed, certainly in Cheshire. John Monfries & Sons is a fine establishment and very good if ever you fancy a trip back in time. I will let the pictures do the talking. The proprietor was kind enough to serve me

everything I needed and then agreed to a photograph in his shop which he duly posed for. I say proprietor but I speculate; he looked like the proprietor as he had an air of authority about him. Maybe this was the son of John Monfries; John junior possibly?

The doorbell jangled as I left with a few modest but essential purchases, one of which was a pint of full-

cream milk which I chugged down in one go after consuming two of my favourite trail snacks: Tunnock's Wafers. None of this energy bar nonsense, I go for the real deal. Particularly when in Scotland.

I stepped back into 2014 and made my way onto the towpath and… not a lot happened until Kirkintilloch. Well that is what my notes suggest. For the first time on this walk the entry in my black incident book (the type that your bobby on the beat uses) is only one side of one page. I usually write the day's happenings from memory in the evening, so it is not as if there was so much grabbing my attention that I did not have time to write. Not easy to do when you are walking anyway.

In actual fact as I mentioned in yesterday's account there was plenty to write about, what with tunnels and rotating canal lifts on the agenda (singular but it sounds better). First structure of note, and not on my list of three, was something of a disappointment. I had noted the 'HM Young Offenders Institution' (in other words a prison) on the map overlooking the canal. I was rather expecting one of those big red-brick Victorian jails with barred windows and turrets everywhere, and perhaps the odd shout of abuse

HM Young Offenders Institution, Polmont

aimed at the lone walker passing by. Once again the reality was very different. The face of the institution presented to the canal side was very plain and very modern, in fact very little to look at all apart from the tallest longest wooden fence I have ever seen. Well it looked like wood. Unlike the modernist garbage in the middle of Linlithgow I digressed on earlier, this was modern with a purpose, and as a result did not offend the eye, well not mine anyway.

Three miles west of Polmont I strode forward quick prison march fashion into Falkirk Tunnel and was immediately impressed. First by its unexpected length and second that it is not lined with brick but hewn out of solid rock. Actually, the whole tunnel was unexpected, as I had not spotted it when planning the walk months earlier; that is because there isn't any 'planning' to do; all you do is follow the towpath for 38 miles; simple! Being familiar with canals and narrowboats I had already been in a few tunnels but this one was something special; the unioncanalunlocked.org.uk website describes it as follows…

Falkirk Tunnel

"This is one of the most atmospheric places on the canal and the longest canal tunnel to be built in Scotland. Once a dark and eerie place, it now has a colourful lighting system that lights your way through 630m of solid rock and highlights the tunnel's features - candle holders, dynamite stores and shafts. Navvies carved and blasted the tunnel through this hillside because the local landowner, William Forbes of Callendar House, campaigned to Parliament against the overland route which would have ruined the view from his house."

Ruined the view?! How does that work Mr Forbes? The line of the tunnel is one mile away from Callendar House so he must have been speculating through a telescope to visualise all those offensive looking boats in the distance. Maybe I am misunderstanding the lie of the land; perhaps the alternative route was via his large duck pond? Who knows; what is clear is that lobbying parliament for personal gain is nothing new. Whatever the case he got his way. Goodbye boats. The only other thing I should mention is the lighting, when I passed through it was a bit more basic, sporadic and as the above description suggests, eerie. In places I was glad of my headtorch with which to pierce the gloom and spot the streaks of water deluging from above. These days some seven years later I imagine that the tunnel is attracting a lot more visitors, with its posh lighting n all as shown on the aforementioned website.

Two miles further along the towpath beyond the north portal of the tunnel the canal takes a sudden hard right ninety-degree turn to the north and enters another tunnel albeit a lot shorter than the one I had just walked through. This tunnel is also a lot newer being purpose built under the railway, road, and hillside to make a beeline for the awe-inspiring Falkirk Wheel which allows boats to be lifted down to the level of the Forth and Clyde Canal. Built as part of the Millennium Link project to reconnect Scotland's great cities of Glasgow and Edinburgh by canal it was opened in 2002 by Her Majesty Queen Elizabeth II as part of her Golden Jubilee celebrations. Read all about it at scottishcanals.co.uk and on Wikipedia; no wisdom in pretending I know it all.

Once emerged from the tunnel something else was unexpected. Whilst I was familiar with the shape and movement of the wheel itself I was not at all aware of the aerial nature of the canal link that connects to it. This is real flying boats territory! All is beautiful modern engineering, sleek but heavy at the same time; proper big boys toys all round, and clearly built to last the 120 year service life it has been designed to deliver; again not a blot and spoiler to the eyes but something that enhances its surroundings. Full marks to all involved, it is functional, well-engineered and beautiful as a result.

Falkirk Wheel

Anyone can freely walk from the Union Canal on the upper level and follow the path down past the back of the visitor centre to a footbridge across the Forth and Clyde Canal on the lower level. If the centre is open then as I did you can also wander around the circular basin and watch the wheel in action. It reminds me more of a bottle opener than a wheel but that's just me. Whatever you make of it, it is an undeniably brilliant thing, and a great replacement for a flight of high maintenance locks that would have taken most of a working day to negotiate.

Blooming Bonnybridge

Beyond the Falkirk Wheel I started to get my first taste of the monotony I mentioned earlier. All is pleasant and green enough alongside the ever present strip of rippling water, but repetition does become the order of the day; until you get to Bonnybridge that is. Just beyond Anderson Park where the houses on Princess Street back on to the canal there is an excellent example of what happens when people care about their surroundings. Suddenly the bland utilitarian tarmac towpath that has been underfoot most of the way from Broxburn is bordered by colourful shrubs, daffodils, tulips, and other plants all lovingly maintained to a high standard. From memory I think it was a memorial garden; I make no mention of it in my notes, so I am not sure. If so it is a beautiful public tribute to whoever prompted its creation. I hope Scottish Canals appreciate this colourful enhancement of their waterfront.

At Bridge Street in Bonnybridge where a modern swing bridge carries the B816 across the canal (there's a lot of bonny and bridge in this part of the world) I paused for a small celebration. I calculated this as my official halfway point, 141 miles behind me since Lindisfarne and the same distance in front to Iona. I wondered if St Aidan celebrated with a handful of nuts and a Tunnock's Wafer. Probably not, he wouldn't have seen the shop.

Bonnybridge marked my halfway point

Just over a mile from Bonnybridge I was greeted by a less bonny sight. Alongside the first of three locks on this stretch of the canal are the derelict remains of what was prior to its destruction The Underwood

Sad remains ~ The Underwood Lockhouse Restaurant

Lockhouse Restaurant. It seemed to me that it had been damaged by fire on the ground floor, but with three-quarters of the roof gone demolition and site clearance seemed inevitable. On my walks I have seen many pubs closed and they are always a sad thing to see, but in most cases closure comes because of changes in Law and the consequences that follow. Tough as that is for all concerned ultimately business has to make money, so things change, and life follows. Here though circumstances were probably very different; I have no idea why such a sad fate befell this establishment, but you can be sure that lives and livelihoods were affected. It was a sad place. I walked on.

Beyond Banknock and where the M80 motorway crosses the canal there are a final few bends before the canal becomes straight, wide, and very monotonous. Phew, I was beginning to think my suggestions of monotony on page 88 were just my imagination and poor memory! I think this was the length of canal I had in mind; I mean look at it; is that not monotony par excellence?

Perspectives on The Forth and Clyde Canal ~ Glasgow or bust!

I sped along towards Kilsyth and my B&B booked near Kirkintilloch, probably occasionally exceeding 3mph, but the convergence of the lines of towpath and canal ever receding into the distance made my destination feel like a forlorn hope. Beyond Kilsyth things improved; with hills closing in on all sides the canal once again took on a more attractive and motivating course, bending and following a contour around the base of Bar Hill at Twechar. It seems the canal engineers on the Forth and Clyde Canal did

not share the same tunnelling instincts of their colleagues on the Union Canal. I was very content to once again be entertained as I wondered what would be around the next bend; there is little mystery in straight lines to the horizon.

I must admit to a degree of relief upon arriving at Bridgend Farm at 4pm. My day's march was over and tomorrow heralded the start of another significant

Bridgend Farm B&B

part of the walk. With more miles behind me than in front of me it was time to mark the occasion with a fish supper.

My host had no hesitation in recommending the local chippy in Kirky (short for Kirkintilloch) so I got on the phone and placed my order accordingly. An unexpected surprise was that the delivery driver did not seem to know where the farm was, despite it being only a mile out of town. He was grateful for my directions and duly arrived at around 6pm whereupon my host directed me to eat at his fabulously large dining table, all set with silverware for breakfast. The man from the chippy handed me my catch and the second surprise hit me; it was very heavy!

My takeaway fish n chips felt about the same weight as a house brick; guess who had forgotten what constitutes a Glaswegian Fish Supper! As directed I took my haul into the dining room and prepared for

The famous Glaswegian Fish Supper ~ the best in the land?

battle. I can tell you now without a breath of hesitation that this was easily the best fish and chips I have ever had, well certainly on this journey anyway. Tragedy was I just could not manage to eat it all; it was truly magnificent and overwhelming at the same time. I had no choice; I was not going to waste this culinary feast, so I asked my host if he would like it. Predictably he had just eaten his tea. "Give it to the crows, put it on the wall, it'll be gone by morning." Again he was not wrong. On all fishy fronts I was comprehensively defeated and so duly, but reluctantly, placed the magnificent battered specimen on the farm wall.

Memo to self: Always remember what constitutes a Glaswegian Fish Supper!

I topped the evening off by repairing my glasses. Once again my host (sadly I do not have his name) came to my rescue and provided a set of jewellers' screwdrivers.

I slept well on a very full stomach. It had been a fine day ending in a fine way.

Tomorrow – the Highlands are calling!

PART FIVE

From Lowlands to Highlands

Kirkintilloch to Inverarnan

Sunday April 27, day 9 • Kirkintilloch to Drymen

It is a particularly galling thought that despite the grandiose title of part five of this book that by the end of it I did not gain a single foot in height (as in the lie of the land; just to be clear and for the avoidance of doubt) in fact I lost a few. Keep that in mind as we proceed…

The morning at Bridgend Farm started with a sumptuous breakfast sat at the same place setting where I had been defeated by the Glaswegian Fish Supper only a few hours earlier. Oddly, the generous fried breakfast seemed to go down well as if I had not eaten well the previous evening. Whilst thinking about it I quickly took a look outside just to double check that the crows had feasted well on the whole piece of five-star battered cod that I had left for them on the wall. Not a scrap to be seen; I mean total wipe-out, not even a crumb of batter left over.

Cre8 ~ Bike Shed

Maybe the sudden restoration of appetite was caused by the fact that I had the pleasure of sharing breakfast with a friend who had travelled up from Macclesfield and was able to join me for the start of today's walk. I introduced Cre8 as this charitable walk's beneficiary on page six; the following paragraphs describe how and why I chose them…

At the time of this walk Jonathan Aiken (Jonny to all who know him) worked for Cre8 Macclesfield, a superb multi-faceted social enterprise organisation based on the Moss Estate in the town, primarily providing one-to-one educational support to youngsters who had for a whole spectrum of reasons been excluded from regular state education.

Cre8 is very close to my heart despite having worked for them only for a short time. I spent a few weeks there as a volunteer and worked with some of the youngsters they were looking after at the time. The work was to say the least challenging, and on reflection something that I did not feel equipped to do. This type of work genuinely requires a calling, as well as professional skill and experience working with disadvantaged kids. All of them deserve the best having had precious little of that so far in their lives. Cre8 provides that in good measure.

This was the first occasion on which I decided to raise money

for charity whilst walking for pleasure, and as described earlier, sometimes with a dash of pain thrown in for good measure. I did not feel under any obligation to become a fundraiser, but it did seem to me that rather than just disappearing for weeks on end and basically having a nice time whilst Janine held the fort back home, I could do something useful at the same time as walking. It just made sense. So I contacted Cre8 and asked if there was a specific project I could help out with. The timing was good because at the time of my enquiry they were embarked on a new project to provide pedal bike servicing and repairs to the local community. Being on a scale that I thought I could realistically support, Cre8's 'Bike Shed' project as it became known was ideal. That is how I came to choose Cre8 as the first charity I would raise money for during one of my walks. More information about Cre8 at cre8macclesfield.org.

Towpath closure in Kirkintilloch ~ modelled by Jonathan Aiken of Cre8

It was a morning of quarter-pasts. I was awake at 5.15am (probably woken by marauding fish-eating crows) up at 6.15am, breakfast at 8.15am and away on the path at 9.15am. Bridgend Farm was an excellent B&B; one for the list. We set off back towards the towpath and I felt strangely light-footed as I bounced along in what must have been an unattractive and ungainly way, this on account of the fact that Jonny had offered to carry my rucksack. What a gentleman!

The day had started grey overcast and cool; another great day for making rapid progress on the canal-side pedestrian highway, although today it would also be time to leave the waterway behind and head north. First objective though was onwards to Kirkintilloch and the land of the world's best chippy! As I type this I can feel my Yorkshire forebears' protests of indignation.

Towpath closures are always annoying, not least today's at Kirkintilloch where Jonny and I were forced into town albeit briefly. As it turned out this one was not a problem, but some I have encountered on my travels have been a real pain, especially when unannounced ahead of time and with no diversions for the pedestrian on offer as I recall happening on my 2018 walk across Lincolnshire. Thankfully, this

Jonny Aiken ~ the very near perfect gentleman!

example was soon behind us and we were back marching with a degree of synchronicity, talking as we went along. Unlike Wainwright I am content with human company when walking, my problem is with over-inquisitive bovines or worse, dogs. Fortunately, I have not had too many encounters with the latter, but they do happen.

Goodbye to Canal Land

At bridge 23 where Cadder Road crosses the canal just outside Bishopbriggs, we three parted company. Jonny headed south to find transport back home and I turned north-west away from the Forth and Clyde Canal towards Milngavie and the start of the West Highland Way.

Upon leaving the canal I immediately faced one of my walking fears, a golf course. This was one of those cases where route planning in Scotland carries uncertainty. I had marked my route to follow alongside Bishopbriggs Burn on the line of a track towards a footbridge over the River Kelvin which turned out to be a private road to the Cawder Golf Club club-house. I was confronted by a 'PRIVATE members only' sign. I felt distinctly unwelcome, so I found, easily as it turns out, an alternative route past Cadder Parish Church. I dislike crossing golf courses anywhere but at least in England, if you have to, you are able to refer to those comforting green or red broken lines indicating your Right of Way. All you have to do then is watch out for lethal flying objects. Golf courses are never pleasant places to be for a hiker.

The Balmore Trust's Coach House café & craft shop

Another recommendation by the same friend that arranged my accommodation in East Calder was to call in at the Balmore Coach House for refreshments. I duly obliged and was once again grateful for advice about facilities that you would otherwise miss out on, and this was a classic case. I stopped for about half-an-hour, had a drink and cake, and read about the work of the Balmore Trust; yet another good example of excellent work being done to support fair trade and help alleviate poverty in various places across the world. More information at balmoretrust.uk

To my dismay I was confronted by a second golf course at Balmore although somehow I managed to avoid any problems. Whatever happened it seemed a much more friendly affair and I soon reached the road beyond feeling quite relaxed. It made a nice change. In Baldernock I was getting my first views back towards the big urban areas around Glasgow with tall tower blocks visible in the misty distance. It felt good to be out of town and to be gradually leaving the urban areas; a sign beckoning me towards Milngavie confirmed that the transition would soon be over.

A sign of progress in Baldernock

Walking into town shortly after noon it felt good to be back in Milngavie. For me this is where all of my solo walking adventures started back in 1999 with that memorable fortieth birthday present courtesy of Janine. Back then I was equipped with my first mobile phone which from memory was a Nokia much like the one shown here. At the time it was about the best you could get without spending the earth. With it you could make phone calls (remember those?) send text messages and, if memory serves me right, you could browse the Internet or what there was of it back then in its embryonic form, if you didn't mind using a screen not much larger than a postage stamp that is. Actually, looking at the picture I think that I am imagining things! One thing I am sure of is that I did not take any photographs with it, for that I used a compact camera loaned to me by my mother-in-law.

Looking towards the high-rise skyline of Glasgow from Baldernock

Milngavie town centre was busy for a Sunday, not that I could judge what it was normally like having only ever been there once before. Although thinking further about this that cannot be true. I definitely started the West Highland Way here in 1999 but I did not see the town centre on that occasion. My first memory was the underpass and very soon after that escaping out of town alongside Allander Water and into Allander Park heading in the direction of the entertainingly named Scroggy Hill, mercifully avoiding Milngavie Golf Course on the way. It all suddenly felt very unfamiliar. Clearly 'developments' had taken place in the 15 years that had elapsed since my last visit. I blame the car parks.

Last time I arrived by train, so having walked through the familiar underpass below Woodburn Way emblazoned with the words 'Welcome to Milngavie' and having already seen a route board outside the

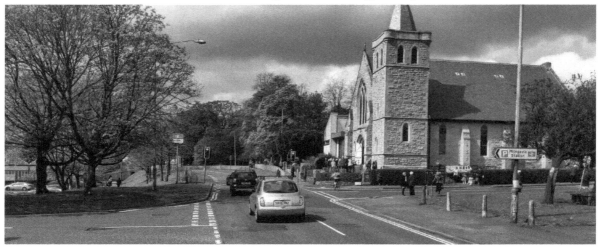

Arrival in Milngavie

Milngavie's memorable underpass and a taste of Washington on Douglas Street at the start of the West Highland Way

pic credit: Calum Christie

railway station, in my head I was back on track; I was at the start of the West Highland Way (initialled WHW hereafter). Let the Highlands commence!

Actually no. Granted it was only a matter of a few hundred yards, but the official WHW start had moved to a very prominent location slap bang in the middle of the main shopping thoroughfare of Douglas Street, and very fine it is too. The old underpass wasn't exactly the most befitting of starts to such a fine route into the Highlands; much better now with the polished Washington Monument obelisk style granite column and accompanying triple span arched banner sign on top of the bridge across Allander Water. Much more the sort of place you would gather for a team picture before embarking on the 96-mile path to Fort William. Well done to the authorities in Milngavie, that is much better. Go teach the things you know to your colleagues in Linlithgow. Please?

It felt great knowing that the most exciting stages of my walk were still to come; the fact that a return to my tent after three consecutive nights in proper accommodation was imminent did not dull my enthusiasm and senses; hills were rising and closing in on my view as once again I passed the wooded slopes of Scroggy Hill.

The West Highland Way just north of Carbeth Loch ~ the prominent hill is called Dumgoyne

On account of its prominence in the landscape and the timing of arrivals on foot starting out from Milngavie, most people walking north will stop for a beer or other refreshment at the large pub on the A81 where the disused railway track as utilised hereabouts by the WHW crosses the road. I called in for a beer and chips at 3.30pm, a bit later than is usual for WHW walkers because I had started my day a lot further away than Milngavie railway station…

Now I do not want to be unkind to the pub in question, but it is one of those establishments that tries to straddle the difficult divide between their two very distinct customer bases. On the one hand they have the walking fraternity and their usual need of things quite basic, and on the other they have those arriving on wheels from the nearby city and suburbs, with all the demands they bring with them; usually for way more than a pint and a chip butty. If like me you do indeed dare to ask for said pint and culinary feast, the result is that you get the distinct and rather unpleasant feeling of getting in the way. Whatever you do, try and avoid using a table either inside or outside that would accommodate a family, that would not go down well. I understand why the pub's proprietors would feel that way and indeed so would I if the pub were mine, but surely there are ways of serving both? Maybe today they have it all sorted, and

everyone is happy; well here's hoping. You will have noticed that I have not named the pub; that is because it is possible that its name has changed more than once. That does tend to happen when you have to reinvent yourself numerous times.

After a very pleasant afternoon's walk on what is one of the easiest sections of the WHW path I arrived at the brilliantly named Easter Drumquhassle Farm otherwise known today by the slightly less interesting commercial name of 'Drymen Camping' in respect of the small town of Drymen a mile or so further north on the route, which on account of the fact that men will from time-to-time turn up at the campsite in a less than dry state, is also quite amusing. Silly of me I know, but true. Well look at the sort of mood I was in; I must have had too much sun or there was something in the beer.

For the first time on the walk I was in the company of other hikers, and it felt good to be in a place where your presence was counted as normal, and worthy therefore of being totally ignored, but in a good way. Walkers generally understand each other well and know that in the case of solo backpackers we are generally content with our own company and are best left to potter pointlessly and pleasantly aimlessly around our tents. If space allows, as it did on this day, then we give each other plenty of it; backpackers know well how far a guttural snore of Hades will travel in the dead of night, as with other noises emitted by the human species.

It was a very peaceful afternoon and as I drifted in and out of sleep towards evening I noticed another first. Evidently, top commanders of the first Highland midge battalions were sending out their early

Camp 6 at Drymen Camping

reconnaissance troops, some of whom were mustering in the top of my flysheet. Hastily I fastened up the inner tent and hid! No one should choose to do battle with the dreaded Highland midge, even with the best of chemical defences in your armoury and about your person they usually win in the end. Thankfully, this early in the season they were not interested (yet) in my sassenach blood.

Monday April 28, day 10 ● Drymen to Cashel

The view towards Loch Lomond from Garadhban Forest

Best night so far under nylon. Tent dry inside and out, weather cool clear and calm with blue skies. With such a fine day in prospect and increasingly long daylight hours plus my planned short day of just 11 miles to Cashel, I felt no compulsion to be anything other than relaxed.

I took time to chat to the campsite owner who admitted that the facilities (ie. the toilet block) were starting to look tired and was looking to improve them for the 2015 season. They seemed fine to me, all clean; just lacking a bit of 'presentation'. When you are on a route that is attracting walkers from around the globe you do have to consider differing levels of expectation, and also the dreaded online reviews which can vary as wildly as the Scottish weather depending upon who is writing them and whether or not a degree of subjectivity rather than objectivity is being applied. Cashel campsite first opened in 1988.

The walk through Garadhban Forest was very different to how I remembered it in 1999 as virtually the whole thing had been harvested for timber. Back then my first view of Loch Lomond was on the ascent of Conic Hill (or chronic hill as some call it) which is the first real hill climb on the WHW, but today the whole glittering expanse of the largest body of water on our island was laid out before me, and mighty fine it looked too. I imagine if I walk the same path for a third time in 2022 that the view may have disappeared again judging by the presence of many deciduous saplings along the way in 2014. Managed forests undergo dramatic changes. If years elapse between visits they are to be expected.

The approach to Conic Hill

Being a few hundred feet above sea level again for the first time since Cauldstane Slap on the Pentland Hills was exhilarating; the realisation that I was at last entering the Highlands proper making it doubly so. The view from the shoulder of Conic Hill across the wide island dotted southern waters of Loch Lomond was expansive and breath-taking. I resisted the temptation to break out into song and instead accelerated down the path towards the lochside, walking poles flaying in all directions.

Loch Lomond seen from Bealach Ard on the descent from Conic Hill

Descent from Conic Hill

Conic Hill was quite busy with people enjoying the climb up from the lochside at Balmaha, a fast-growing tourist centre for activities on and around the loch. I talked to a few folk on the way including an elderly couple from Holland and a fella from Brisbane on his first visit to our "small country" as he was seemingly keen to point out. He was like me a solo walker; I hoped his big country mentality would not dull his grasp of distance, the size of things, and our place among them. Granted Australia is huge compared to our island of Great Britain, but so often you discover that any size awareness people express is from an aircraft or maybe a car, but rarely on foot. Of course there are people that walk huge distances making my efforts seem paltry, but ultimately it is not big numbers that matter, rather more important is perception of our own presence in the landscape; that is what really counts. Knowing the effort it takes to move on foot across an island and to appreciate that as humans we really are very small in the vastness and context of Creation is what is important to me.

I think I have at last started to 'size up' Great Britain; modest in size compared to others maybe, but for me just right. I am pleased to be both English and British and to be able to call this island my home.

Arriving down at the lochside came the realisation that I had just lost all that height gained, but it did not matter, with a new expanse of water before me Lindisfarne suddenly felt a lot further behind me than the miles that I had walked; memories of those first few steps across the Causeway were already beginning to seem distant. Time plays some very strange tricks on the mind, particularly when away from home I find. Have you ever noticed how the first half of a holiday week or more can seem to last for a deliciously long time and then once past the midway point the remainder passes all too quickly?

Closing in as I was on 200 miles walked since the start I felt determined to savour these latter stages as I made my way towards the west coast. Once away from the bustle around Balmaha I drifted through the woodlands heading north as if in dreamland, happily dwarfed by magnificent Scots pines with the sound of the waters lapping onto the pebbly shoreline with a resiny aroma in the air. I may not have been high as in height, but I think I was high in other ways. I arrived at an almost deserted Cashel campsite at 1.30pm and quickly pitched my tent beside the stream.

Cashel is a large campsite rambling along the Loch Lomond shoreline; the beauty and tranquillity of its setting is undeniable. Sadly on this occasion, coincident with the pushing in of my final tent peg, the peace was shattered by a JCB tractor, jack hammer and strimmer trio singing in unholy harmony.

Queen Elizabeth Forest Park

The workmen had finished their lunch and had resumed operations clearing ground and knocking timber posts deep into the ground. All necessary work I guess but the timing was a tad unfortunate; had I arrived a few minutes later I would have pitched my tent at the other end of the site.

I escaped the mechanical hullabaloo by throwing all my gear in the tent to have a carefree wander along the shore. All at once I was unaware of the noise, perhaps they had stopped, or was it just that the peace was louder? I could not believe that there I was seemingly with the whole of Loch Lomond to myself.

It was glorious, the water itself being calm and still, like shimmering glass. Temptation was there to go for the full-on wild swimming thing, but I had mercy on anyone that may have been in the vicinity and chose to paddle instead. The cooling balm of the cold water was intense and just what I needed to calm the troubling aches and pains within my right shin that I had first started to feel at Drymen after three consecutive long days mainly along a solid towpath. Again the military boots I was wearing were taking their toll, but at the time I did not suspect them because they were on the whole

Feeling tranquil

Loch Lomond

comfortable and, critically, kept my feet dry; but as I mentioned at the end of part three it was the soles and their complete lack of a forgiving resilience within them that were the problem. Evidence of my blisters that had troubled me a week ago were fast disappearing only to be replaced by another that would not resolve itself until near Oban. Oh hindsight, I say again: you are just so beautiful.

Substantively chilled I made my way back to the campsite reception and collected my mail packet from home containing the maps I needed for the rest of the walk and to pay for the ones I had finished with to be sent back home. The potential for these things getting lost is a concern that always looms larger in my mind than it should. Having supply boxes and packets arrive from a complete stranger posted to addresses that you do not live at always feels risky, but the system has never failed me, except once perhaps when I nearly forgot to collect. I always prearrange these deliveries but

Camp 7 at Cashel

when sending to post-offices or as in this case a busy reception there is always that outside chance that A does not talk to B. Happily, my concerns are thus far unfounded.

I got talking to the men who were working on site with their trio of instruments. The conversation moved perhaps unwisely to the subject of Scottish independence something that I have never been in favour of, but what do I know, I am English! It took less than a few seconds into this subject matter to determine that they were firmly in favour of an independent Scotland "...free of those parasites in Westminster!" was a term I seem to recall. We moved on and talked about the fence they were installing.

Two Russian guys turned up later in the afternoon and pitched up a few yards away. Well I say 'pitched up' but that is not actually what happened, it was more of, how do I put this, a 'stealthy' approach. I was not spying on my neighbours or anything like that you understand but I could not help but notice the order of things. First a large rectangular groundsheet was stretched out on the grass and weighted down with all their gear, not in a temporary fashion but in an unpacked 'finished sleeping arrangements' way. Then they started cooking a meal; wisps of smoke drifted up into the still early evening air followed by the poetic sounds of Russians in conversation in a language I am very familiar with but have little understanding of. An hour or so later a pole was erected in the middle of their territory and a large silver tarpaulin was stretched out to all four corners with a gap of about eighteen inches all around, and that was them, a little bit of Russia planted in Scotland. I ventured over to have a chat.

Albeit within the constraints of mutual language difficulty I found my two Russian camping companions, one of whom was called Andrei, friendly and approachable, I even dared to utter a few of words of

Russian taken from my exceedingly limited vocabulary. Like me they were walking north on the WHW. We laughed, that was the main thing. If you can laugh together then you are human together, no other barriers matter; except perhaps one to defend against the ever more excitable midges. May was approaching.

I was impressed with the Russian approach to camping or at least this example of it. Personally, I am not really into the whole 'tarps' thing, especially considering the local winged residents soon to take flight in armed hungry-for-blood legions. With that thought and with the sounds of faraway lands in my mind I returned to my tent and once again drifted off into dreamland; this time horizontal and with eyes closed.

Tuesday April 29, day 11 ● Cashel to Inverarnan

Loch Lomond from Cashel

I woke up to a classic highland morning. The air was intoxicatingly clear but aromatic with a light mist lazily rising from the loch and cloud spilling off the nearby mountains like a bedraggled quilt. With the dawn of this fine new day, scenery to die for and the promised return of the JCB trio, I decided to move on. Cashel is a gorgeous place to be but better without the hubbub of machinery and pro-independence workers to enliven the ambience.

Despite only modest heights being gained and lost during today's 19-mile walk to Inverarnan, day 11 was to be the toughest so far on my route and is generally also regarded as such on the WHW. The route follows the eastern shoreline of Loch Lomond but is never quite on it, choosing instead to twist and turn on the wooded boulder-strewn slopes hillocks and knolls above it like a game of snakes and ladders, with the all the ups and downs that that game involves. A crescendo of complexity is reached in the vicinity of Ptarmigan Lodge a mile to the north of Rowardennan as the path skirts the base of Ben Lomond, with the boulder and tree-root infested 'entertainment' continuing for some miles to the head of the loch at

The WHW in Ross Wood

Ardleish, where the path becomes more of a pleasure and less of a battle.

All was quiet on the Russian front as I decamped, got underway and faced the first unplanned challenge of the day on the Ross Wood headland, where somehow I must have deviated off the WHW path and ended up doing battle with the dense forest. I was catching glimpses of water on all sides clearly indicating that I was both lost and possibly going round in circles desperately trying to regain the path. Being properly disorientated in a forest is one of the most unnerving feelings you can have. I was not in any danger but that is not how I felt as I regained the path having added an hour and an unnecessary mile to the route. On this occasion my GPS device was of little use, I found my own way, eventually.

By the time I reached it at about 1pm (perfect timing) the bar at the Inversnaid Hotel was open, so I ventured inside and bought a pint of Belhaven bitter. To my dismay food was not on offer, so I made do with a couple of bags of crisps and a big chunk of sickly-sweet carrot cake to be supplemented with my onboard supplies. I sat down on the hotel jetty with my makeshift lunch and watched the pleasure craft skim by on the

Looking across to the youth hostel from the jetty at Rowardennan with the slopes of Ben Lomond rising beyond

Inversnaid Hotel

now agitated waters of the loch, sharing a wave or two with the passengers as they hurried along on their watery way.

For reasons unknown I always confuse Inversnaid with Rowardennan which, following the WHW, is all of seven miles to the south. The two are in fact very different; Inversnaid is dominated by the substantial hotel which takes its name and is the only building serving the public in the area, whereas Rowardennan is fast becoming a lakeside resort like Balmaha and Luss in the south, with at least two hotels, self-catering lodges, a boat yard, piers, moorings, attendant waymarked trails, and a large car park. Another key difference is the road access, Rowardennan being served by a good road from Drymen to the south with direct highway connections to Alexandria and Glasgow beyond, whereas Inversnaid is served by minor roads from Aberfoyle to the east which for much of their length are single track with passing places. I hope they stay that way and thus preserve this classic highly regarded hotel in its beautiful lochside location. I am hoping one day to be able to afford to stay there.

Having ate my fill I rolled the dice and continued north. The walking seemed harder and longer than during my first 'birthday present' encounter in

Ben Arthur and the Arrochar hills seen from near Inversnaid

Looking across Loch Lomond from Inversnaid towards Inveruglas and Ben Vane

Scrambles, slithers, squeezes, ladders and maybe even snakes ~ all part of the Loch Lomond WHW experience!

1999. Maybe it was the intervening birthdays that were taking their toll on my mind and legs. Looking across to the other side of the loch the view changed stubbornly slowly giving me the unsettling feeling that my progress was even slower than I thought. But change it did and soon enough I was seeing snow

Someone mention ladders?

on the Arrochar Hills as the Highlands started to assert their presence. My progress was fine, I was just impatient for more, to see the next amazing view. The Highlands were working their magic, once you are hooked they never let you go.

Near a location on the 1:25,000 Ordnance Survey map marked 'Smuggler's Cave' of which there seems to be very little evidence on the ground, you leave the lochside and start climbing away from the water's edge, and unless you check yourself you will feel, as I did back in 1999, that you have reached the head of Loch Lomond and that the end of a long day is near. Sadly, this is a false perception, because ahead are the longest three miles I know, at the end of which is the Beinglas campsite at Inverarnan. I do not know what it is about false dawns or why they occur, but this is a classic. In the bigger scheme of things three miles more is not such a big deal when you have already covered a modest sixteen, but when a good proportion of those sixteen miles have had as much up and down motion in them as a Highland fling, three miles can seem a very long way indeed. There have been scrambles, slithers on muddy slopes and even a squeeze between trees along the way where backpacks of any size have to be removed to get through. It has been an action packed day, and like many northbound walkers on the WHW before and after me, I am feeling the need for rest well before the day is done.

Doune and the view north towards Ben Lui

As a walker on the WHW it is easy to understand why the road on the western shore of Loch Lomond evolved to become the main route linking Glasgow and the south with the Highlands. North of Tarbert the A82 road engineers continue to be confounded when considering road widening and improvement. What is certain is that the challenges would have been even greater had time favoured the eastern shore where the obstacles are in places difficult even for backpackers to negotiate. These days in engineering terms all is possible, but at what cost? Thankfully, from a visual point of view the scale of the countryside hereabouts is such that man's greatest achievements in this regard are but shiny thin ribbons; tiny intrusions set against a magnificent backdrop of beauty. Walking north towards Inverarnan where the loch narrows you become increasingly aware of the road on the opposite shore. Were it not for the hum of the traffic you would not know it was there.

Having faced the illusion of arrival at the day's premature end in the past, this time round I was not deceived and instead concentrated my attention on the sylvan beauty that lay ahead; at Doune superlatives fail. It is indeed true that the further north you go along Loch Lomond the more enchanting it becomes. There is beauty here that can make a grown man cry and consider his Maker. Here is humility. Here, if you look for it, you find your peace and feel truly alive.

Look deep into the flower of a common primrose and you can see everything that holds the universe together. Look again, the design is perfect in every way. Before I go 'off on one' here I will ground myself by also noting the full Latin name: *Primula vulgaris*. Apparently 'vulgaris' means 'common' as in widespread. I would have named it magnificent. It seems I was born too late.

Woolly watchers not watching but ignoring me

Common primrose

Beyond Doune the path descends back down to the shoreline of the loch with Ardlui and the true head of Loch Lomond in sight. Hereabouts near Ardleish is the opportunity to call a pedestrian ferry from the other side of the loch by means of an orange ball that you can raise up a white pole to summon the service "AT ALL TIMES" as the sign on the pole declares. Apparently the service is run by the Ardlui Hotel presumably to give visitors a taste of the other quieter side of the loch or maybe to do a bit of hiker spotting.

From the WHW walker's point of view on first consideration the service might seem pointless being so near the end of the loch, surely you could walk round? But then you have to consider the River Falloch

pic credit: Douglas Taylor

Ardleish ferry terminal

Ardlui and the head of Loch Lomond seen from Ardleish

which feeds the loch and the fierce and deadly waterway that it can become. Bearing all this in mind you need no further convincing of the merits of the ferry, especially if you are marooned on the Ardleish side without a tent or Beinglas Campsite is booked to the hilt as it often can be in high season. My Russian friends came back to mind, I had not seen them all day. Perhaps they were more tolerant of the

Last view of Loch Lomond looking south from Cnap Mor

Four-bed camping cabin at Beinglas campsite

mechanically progressive music at Cashel than I was and had opted to stay. I hoped they were not lost and were alright. I liked them. Nice lads.

I arrived in Inverarnan at Beinglas campsite at 5pm and hired a cabin for two nights, more out of curiosity than need. In the 15 years that had elapsed since I last pitched my tent here the site had grown beyond all recognition. What was little more than a field beside a farmhouse in 1999 had become a fully facilitated camping ground for tents of all shapes and sizes including a range of two and four-person camping cabins; a shop, café and all the usually expected amenities to complete the picture. What had not changed was its height above sea level. After all the rigours of the day I was astonished to discover that I was actually lower than I was when I left the farm at Kirkintilloch. So much for 'Lowlands to Highlands'!

To this day I cannot say 'Inverarnan' without recalling one evening at the old Drovers Inn back in 1999 on the WHW...

I had taken up residence on a tall stool at the bar. After eating a generous platter of fish chips and veg and downing two pints of the local brew, the evening thereafter melted into a fuzzily happy haze, fuelled by copiously generous servings of the best single malt whisky I had ever had. The landlord (at least that was who I assumed him to be) was a giant of a man in full Highland dress complete with tartan kilt, sporran, sgian-dubh and Doc Marten boots. His whisky measures were as big as his character. The golden 'uisge beatha' overflowed the pewter measure down on to the planished and polished copper bar top flowing in all directions. Combine this with the huge roaring fire, a stuffed bear stood reared up on two feet in the entrance, Highland weapons of war plus other memorabilia hung on the beamed walls and ceiling, a dreich night outside resulting in standing room only plus all the attendant noise of human banter to go with it... all this added together with the aromas from whisky and fire, made for an atmosphere that was thick and delicious.

I lost count of how many whiskies I had; all I know that I had difficulty back at the campsite. I found plenty of tents and tried the entrance to a few. I think mine was the fifth one I tried, or at least I think it was mine. Whatever, I went inside and remember nothing more. That was a very good night indeed. Trussy was a little 'merry' to say the least. With these happy memories in mind I settled down in one corner of my wooden hutch for four. I slept very well and dreamt of Mac and Mc Clans, ancient battles, fire, and whisky. Tomorrow was to be my postponed rest day and maybe a chance for a return visit to the infamous Drovers Inn!

Sunset at Beinglas campsite

TIME TO REST

Recuperation in Inverarnan

Another Rest Day ~ Going nowhere and talking about boots

Wednesday April 30 ● Rest Day 3

Beinglas campsite entrance

It quickly became evident that another rest day was in order. It was planned anyway at Cashel but for reasons explained earlier I postponed it. Inverarnan, with all the memories it held of a long time ago seemed the right place to stop and give my increasingly troublesome right leg chance to recover from the pounding of the last week. My blisters had all but healed up with reinforced skin which was gradually replacing the soft housebound heels that I walked on for the first few days.

Nowadays I wander house and garden at home with bare feet and have been doing so now for a number of years. It is interesting to watch your feet age like your face, not the most pleasant spectacle, but they are a lot more resilient now and find it far less 'shocking' when I suddenly embark on a long walk. This combined with finding a type of ex-military boot with a more resilient sole and also investing in proper insoles to go in them is transforming my walking experience. Why does it take me so long to learn these basics I ask myself...

Time for a deliberate digression on the subject of BOOTS...

I have had two pairs of 'proper' all leather upper walking boots in recent years made by Scarpa, by all accounts a manufacturer of some renown. Having endured the lessons of this walk I invested in a pair for my 2016 walk from Lowestoft to Land's End; they were £110 but a penny and made in the sturdy eastern European country of Romania; a place I know well. They looked excellent and felt great on when new but early on in that walk I noticed my right foot getting damp, and it was more than just sweat and toil. At the end of my 2016 walk after well over 500 miles, and a number of times being dried out and then wetted again, the leather on the right boot had failed as examination upon returning home had

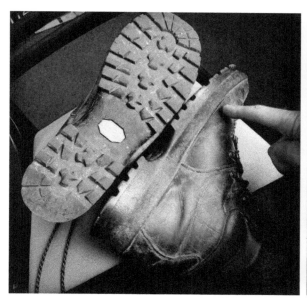

revealed. I was criticised by the retailer (who shall remain nameless but it's the big one that trades out of warehouses on retail parks) for not maintaining them properly and "…allowing the leather to dry out…". I explained 'maintaining them properly' midway on a 500-mile solo hike was not practicable, especially when on many occasions you are depending on your host's help and generosity to dry your stuff after a long wet day outside. In any case these were not cheap boots, at the price they were one expected a little more resilience and durability regardless of what life on and off the path threw at them.

Thankfully Scarpa came to my rescue and supplied a replacement pair via the said retailer. Clearly they recognised defective sub-standard leather in the boot and acted accordingly with no comment about how I had maintained the boots. Top marks to Scarpa; fewer marks to the retailer who perhaps should give more of a hearing to the voice of experience when they hear it.

The pair shown here were used for my 2018 and 2019 walks and have been a lot better having withstood use and abuse for well over 2 years and at least 1000 miles on these two journeys and other day trips out; but they too eventually showed signs of leather fatigue in much the same way as the first pair although this time, admittedly, after a much longer period. I have carried out my own 'refurbishment' of these which has been surprisingly effective considering that all I have done is paste the weak areas of leather over with one of those gun-applied black rubber compounds that is commonly used for building yachts, narrowboats, caravans, and other leisure vehicles. So far my 'fix' has worked like a dream.

Boot parade! ~ L to R old ex-military (this 2014 walk), replacement Scarpas (2018/19/22), new ex-military (2022)

In addition to repairing my Scarpa boots I now have a second pair of ex-military boots of a different design to the ones I used on this 2014 walk, which as I have intimated already, were the reason for all my injury troubles between Lindisfarne and Iona. They are very much better with a build plus leather quality which really is in another league. They are clearly a different generation of boot, designed to be a little more forgiving in service whether in the military or civilian sense.

I use ex-military boots because of the generally superior build quality and design features which is particularly innovative in the cut of the one-piece leather upper. Also, being second hand, they have the benefits of being both pre worn-in and by being substantively cheaper than my Scarpas; by £50 at the time of purchase. Admittedly I have not used the latest pair for a long-distance walk yet (I bought them in 2020 in preparation for my next attempt on Cape Wrath from the south coast; now postponed for a second time to 2022 because of the pandemic) so the real test is yet to come but having used them regularly in recent times I am feeling much more confident about their suitability and durability – especially with my newly toughened up feet inside them. The soles of these newer ex-military boots are a special Vibram "Tsavo" design. Well it sounds pretty special to me; they have to be when designed for the German military! They are also fully Gore-Tex lined and certified as a working boot to European Standard EN ISO 20347. So there! Absolutely no excuses for failure or pain!

Here endeth the BOOTS section. Time to get back to Inverarnan…

I felt rather cocooned at Inverarnan. Compared to my tent the cabins were cavernously spacious; they were also clean, dry, and well insulated both thermally and acoustically; but as a result of all this, especially if the weather is as wet as it became today, you start to feel a bit isolated, especially if solo. This feeling of confinement increased when the campsite owner asked me to move from the four-bed cabin to a two-bed. I assumed the four-bed was given me because it was the only one available at the time and now it was needed for a larger party. All fair enough although a bit of a pain having to move just for one night.

Two-bed camping at Beinglas campsite

I spent the morning poring over the maps that Janine sent to Cashel to familiarise myself as much as I could with the high level routes to come between Inverarnan and Oban. All routes were pre-planned, but you cannot beat spreading out the maps on the floor and visualising the landscape, especially bearing in mind the very limited area of map that can be seen on a GPS. All these years later in 2021 with much-improved devices this remains the main limitation of these technologies, so a degree of familiarity with the route beyond a strip of cartography either side of it can only be a good thing.

Sleep is also a good thing, so during the afternoon I took the opportunity to catch up on some. For that purpose, the cabins score a solid ten out of ten. I also called the Portsonachan Hotel on Loch Awe to confirm my stay for one night and a boat across the loch. It was a good job that I did. Apparently the person that had taken my booking some months earlier had left. Somewhat alarmingly, today's receptionist had no record of what was, for me, a critical-path stopover. I repeated my booking requests; thankfully, there was still room, and a boat.

Come the evening there was only one thing to do; return to the Drovers. In the fading light and now persistent rain I made my way across the bridge, over the lively waters of the River Falloch, and walked the short half mile to the inn. From the outside little had changed but stepping once again through the front doors, things were very different. In the entrance hall the stuffed bear had gone (these days probably a good thing) and all looked a little bare. Through the doors to the left was the bar that I had such a memorable time in on my previous visit. All was still very nice, although on that dreich night back in 1999 'nice' was not a word that would have come immediately to mind; 'earthy' perhaps would have been a better description. The bar seemed lower than I remembered it and the copper top had gone so that must have been replaced; also the fire was an enclosed log-burner not the ember spitting fiery dragon that I remembered.

In the tough economic times of the early twenty-first century change must come. I understand that. If I had the responsibility of running a catering hotel establishment doubtless I would have to do the same. It must be really tricky striking the right balance with families of all types, often on a long journey north or south, wanting a full weekday lunchtime menu on the one hand, and the drink-til-you-drop (not me of course) type clientele who might be staying in the hotel or may have ambled across from the nearby campsite. I enjoyed that night in the bar in '99 but not everyone likes the experience of packing in like sardines and fighting your way to the bar saying endless 'scuse me's to order your food and drink.

The Drovers Inn

Rant alert!

Where I do draw the line though is manifest in this one word: gastropub. For me food is not an opportunity to create a piece of sculpture that I am about to eat. Also I liked it served on a plate not on a lump of wood or slate; I mean surely that cannot be a superior solution to the glazed ceramic plate in terms of hygiene? As for them being square instead of round – grrrrrrr…

I am sure the Drovers will be loved by many, and indeed I am looking forward to visiting it again, but I do hope I feel more welcome when I do. On this occasion dressed in my hiking gear and boots I felt distinctly unwelcome. Maybe it was just me. After sitting down at a table and looking at the menu for five minutes I left and went back to the campsite. It was not the menu that put me off it, it was the atmosphere (or lack of it) and the prices. Shame really.

I walked back in the now pouring rain to the campsite and bought some food from the shop. I prepped and ate it back in the cabin and turned in for the night. It had been a boring day, but I thanked God that I had got some rest and avoided the rain. Small mercies.

PART SIX

High Ways & Water Ways

Inverarnan to Oban

Thursday May 1, day 12 ● Inverarnan to Dalmally

Contemplation of high places from Inverarnan

Most of my walks are done solo. That on account of the fact that I am in a family minority of one when it comes to walking a long way with rucksack and shelter on my back. I can understand why; hiking is not everyone's 'cup of tea' and is not always enjoyable, in fact sometimes it can become a bit of a drudge and even risky, although most of my walks are designed to be as risk free as possible. With advancing years I do not want to invite trouble, and even less want to waste the time of our magnificent mountain rescue services by making foolish decisions to walk in wild country without properly assessing the risks, or worse, ignoring them. Most of the time however, despite perhaps in the view of some being over cautious, after every journey, no matter how modest in its ambition, I feel a great sense of achievement and ever greater connection with my island home.

As I contemplated the next stage of this walk over high ground towards Oban and Mull beyond, I felt a great sense of anticipation and a degree of apprehension because I was about to enter some very wild country, about as uninhabited as anywhere on this island. Gazing out of the camping cabin the sky hung heavy and grey with water; it had not stopped raining in over twenty-four hours. The day was to start in a characteristically damp Highland manner; although with the dawning of a new month, my third week on route and 200 miles behind me, I felt optimistic. Also it was time to leave the West Highland Way and head west. I finished an inadequate and over-priced breakfast in the campsite café and got going...

Crossing the River Falloch for the last time I stepped onto the quiet A82 road and turned right, away from the Drovers to face north. Technically being the rush hour this could have been a tricky mile, but the road was quiet without any of the traffic hazards that might be expected, in fact I don't have any recollection of a single vehicle passing me between the campsite and where I turned onto the track.

Access rights or wrongs?

Today's first obstacle was a clutch of heavy padlocks on the gate giving access to the hills on what turns out to be an access track for Scottish Water and others, the sort of thing that has a distinct air of 'go away you're not welcome here' stamped all over it, or less polite words to that effect. This is a great example of the problem with the Law in Scotland on the subject of access. On the one hand the Law gives me the right to wander anywhere on the hills and the land owner can fall on the wrong side of said Law if they prevent me from doing so, much like a land owner south of the border has a duty to keep Rights of Way open and accessible. On the other hand a land owner apparently has the right to control who accesses their land. Hence the padlocks.

I climbed over the gate and walked uphill away from the road as quick as I could, not wanting any chance of a 'debate' with anyone locally. Access to this track, which would take me across the pass to the southwest of Ben Lui (Beinn Laoigh) and Beinn a' Chleibh, was a key part of my planned route. Denial of access would have meant a significant addition of miles and time via Crianlarich and Tyndrum, with a lengthy road walk along the busy A85 road. Much as it pains me to say my walks have to be planned,

Gleann nan Caorann

Wild country working ~ water pipeline and pylons in utilitarian harmony

Water intake 'bunker'

and envisaged routes must be adhered to where and whenever possible, otherwise paid work at home would never get done.

Once on the track progress was good. It is an undeniable fact that steady rain is not what you would wish for on a long walk but with the solid ground of the track underfoot and with a coat on that just about kept me dryish I really could kick on. Stops to look at views and take pictures are few and far between because what you can see is limited by the interminable greyness of the day. Undeterred I strode meaningfully forward zigzagging with the track up the slopes of Troisgeach Bheag, the hill which guards the entrance to Gleann nan Caorann beyond, wondering if the rain might consider relenting before the end of the day at Dalmally.

Before long there is the first of a long line of ugly concrete structures built deeply into the hillside alongside the track, many of which look like military bunkers. On closer examination, and at risk of losing my mobile phone as I peered into one its dark openings using its feeble torch, I discovered that they are in fact a long line of stream intakes presumably feeding a hidden water pipeline. As with any other utilitarian infringement on this walker's hoped-for nirvana, I always bear in mind that without these water-collecting structures, pylons, or the increasing number of wind turbines, we would not have a modern economy…

Water management in particular always deserves understanding and respect. Beyond the intakes the pipeline is exposed as it crosses a tributary in the valley head to intersect with a line of pylons that stride up from Troisgeach Bheag for over five miles up the glen, heading like me towards Glen Orchy in unflinching straight line precision. I am conscious that I am not painting a very attractive picture of Gleann nan Caorann; that is because picturesque is not an attribute that readily comes to mind hereabouts. This is wild country, but it also serves a purpose, one we all depend on.

The headwaters of Allt a' Mhinn with Meall nan Tighearn and Gabhar beyond

At last and quite surprisingly the rain stopped as I arrived at the bealach (pass) to the south of Beinn a' Chleibh and just above and to the east of the old shielings called Airigh a' Chaorainn. Shielings are a collection of basic upland dwellings that were used in the past by farming families to graze their livestock on common land during the summer months.

I hope that your appreciation of Scottish Gaelic is developing as you read this; apart from a basic understanding of its pronunciation I know little about it as a spoken language, but I include the names as I find them on Ordnance Survey maps, so you have an idea of my location as I walk in these more obscure parts of the Highlands.

As I picked my way across the featureless moor of the watershed dodging numerous lochans and pools, memories of the Pennine Way and my first adventures into wild country came to mind. For me, these landscapes whilst not unique in the world are a key characteristic of Great Britain; high windswept areas of moorland, devoid of trees, unattractive to both development and farming; scorned by many as being ugly and unworthy of attention and lacking obvious beauty, such as that which adorns the English Lake District. Wainwright did not like the Pennine Way, but he appreciated it for its 'differences' all the same.

With the rain stopped and the air clearing below the cloud base, which was up at around 700 metres, the

view beyond the bealach opened up with dramatic effect. Suddenly Ben Cruachan seemed close when in reality it was still 10 miles away. Just beyond the top of the pass I looked back at a substantial signpost indicating that I had just left the 'Ben Lui National Nature Reserve'. Clearly they did not expect any visitors to negotiate the padlocked gate in Glen Falloch and approach from the direction I had just walked. Well whatever the rights and wrongs of access from Glen Falloch, I hereby defer to Scotways because the route I was following features as route 103 in their book as mentioned at the beginning of part three. It is really odd how sometimes you cannot shake off feelings of unease even when the Law is on your side!

The shelter of the forest came as a relief after the exposure of the bleak open expanses of the bealach although I felt thankful that the wind had remained behind me all the way, still blowing from the east as it was.

Everything was green again, even luminescent in places. Evidence of recent high winds was once again manifested in fallen trees strewn across the track on the descent down to Succoth Lodge, beyond which I passed under the Oban to Crianlarich railway. From there the gradient eases

Looking west towards the Ben Cruachan massif and Beinn Eunaich at the head of Loch Awe

Fallen trees and clover carpets in the vicinity of Succoth Lodge

and an easy walk on a forestry track follows down to the main A85 road at Corryghoil. Even after only six hours in wild country, being back in the land of tarmac, white lines and signs had a feeling of security about it, false though that may be. Perhaps it is just the presence of the familiar. Walking partly on the road and partly on the generous grass verges, the last mile-and-a-half of the day's hike ended in Dalmally village a short distance away from my planned camp site alongside the River Orchy at Dalmally Bridge.

Slow down! Dalmally

I did not intend to visit the gift shop but then again I was not expecting tartan shortbread, small souvenir pots of jam and 'wish u were here' cards in an apparently ordinary workaday village; all I saw was the word 'Open' displayed in a door and a postman's bike hung high up on the wall under a Post Office sign. As it happens the man behind the counter was really helpful not least in filling my Platypus water bladder (backpackers will know what this is) and advising a good place to camp by the river; he also kindly directed me to Glenview Store, the real village shop. I expressed my thanks, selected a packet from the vast array of shortbread choices, and went on my way.

Glenview Stores topped up the rest of my depleted provisions. Feeling well prepared for a night back in the tent I duly celebrated with an Oreo Cornetto which was up there in the top five sweetest things I have ever tasted. Suitably enlivened by this sugar and cream substitute overdose I made my way to the river gaining access from the road opposite Glenorchy Parish Church.

In the pages of a book like this it is all too easy to overuse superlative words like 'idyllic' and thus far, hopefully, I have avoided doing so. However camp eight was, truly, idyllic, beautiful, serene. Take your pick; it was all of them. After the wild openness of the high bealach crossing from Inverarnan it was the perfect stopover. I was so taken with the exclusiveness of my chosen site that inadvertently, with an apparent desire to tumble into the River Orchy in my PJs in the small hours of the morning, I pitched my tent way too close to the crumbling embankment. I moved it. Being swept helplessly away towards Loch Awe in the middle of the night was not my idea of fun.

Here it is time for a photographic break. Yes I know there have been a lot of them already but hereabouts I was truly trigger happy, so in the interest of brevity, and keeping superlatives to a minimum, I will let the pictures speak for themselves with unbroken voice. There are other stories to tell before I leave here.

Pictures on facing page are of camp 8 (versions 1 & 2) vicinity and the beginnings of
Dalmally Community Orchard including rock garden and bug hotel!

Championship skimmers

Dalmally Bridge over the River Orchy ~ and the view from it of stone skimming heaven!

Suddenly and unexpectedly an alien noise interrupted the gentle sounds of the river. On the phone it was none other than my eldest brother Dave telling me that they were going to meet me on Iona. Talk about happy; tears of joy were in evidence accompanied by some very worrying parental dancing. I did not care a hoot. Best news on the walk so far.

To celebrate I went down to the pebble beach for a session of stone skimming par excellence. I am in no way the world's best, likely not even a Truswell best being uncle to Joe 'The Touch' Truswell who is a drumming and skimming legend in his own right; nevertheless skim I did for a happy hour using an endless stock of perfect stones. Surely this should be a training venue for the world championships at Easdale Island?

I was joined by a young lad from Oban (he told me he was born there) with his dog Sammy who was intent on recovering all the stones I cast over the water; he was a very good swimmer. The boy was keen, not to outclass me with his stone-skimming ability, but to demonstrate use of the rope swing which was

Winter persisting on Beinn Eunaich (above) ~ Edendonich with Ben Cruachan in the distance (below)

hooked up into a tree that was overhanging the swirling waters. Without hesitation he was spinning and gyrating at an alarming angle, at the same time laughing and goading me to push him higher. Sensing impending disaster I thought better of it and let him come to rest dangling over the water; unable to get back without a swim. Back up at my tent I grabbed a walking pole, extended it to full length, and hauled in the catch. Great lad. I didn't think to ask his name. I did not know I would be writing about him in seven years' time… Sammy and his owner went on their way back to the village where I assumed he lived, and I went for a walk to explore the local area and get a few more snaps, as if I had not taken enough already. Of all the places I had so far stopped on this journey this was by far the most photogenic with ready-framed views abounding on all points of the compass.

I walked over the bridge to spy out the small communities of Edendonich and Stronmilchan with houses old and new strung out in happy disarray along the old military road, and also to get a better look at Ben Cruachan which filled the view beyond still some miles away. At nearly 3,700 feet high the Ben is not so much one mountain as a range of mountains, all deserving of respect. In the context of this east to west

Glenorchy war memorial

journey getting past the Cruachan massif involved some difficult choices, so much so that I wrote specifically to Scotways about it, and they were kind enough to respond at some length, agreeing with many of my concerns…

Copied on the opposite page, the letter reply I received from Scotways explains in detail. In short, alternatives were either going round Ben Cruachan via a long diversion and a high pass to the north, a potentially deadly walk accompanied by juggernauts and tourist coaches along the notorious Pass of Brander to its south, or over the top (literally) via its lofty summit. There was however one other choice which, after many hours of head-scratching and wondering what St Aidan may have done in pre-mediaeval times, became the only choice: a boat across Loch Awe. This was the most important decision in the whole route plan and was key to making this journey practicable in the given time, and a good excuse for a bit of unadulterated luxury!

Crossing back over the bridge across the River Orchy I stopped briefly at the local war memorial recognising and reminding me of the cost of war to communities far and wide, whether urban or rural it is of the highest order to both. Duly and thankfully I paid my respects.

ScotWays®   *The Scottish Rights of Way and Access Society*

16/12/13.

Dear Paul,

This sounds an exciting expedition; is it a kind of "pilgrimge"?

But, of course, there is no way across Loch Awe and a certain amount of road walking seems inevitable.

From Oban, instead of taking Route 108 to Kilchrenan, I'd consider walking along the minor road through Glen Lonan to Taynuilt. This road is quiet and scenic and I've used it on a cross-Scotland cycle route from Oban.

From Taynuilt, the Pass of Brander is horrific and walking over Cruachan seems mega-masochistic. I don't know what it would be like walking round the north side of Cruachan and up Glen Noe. It looks as though it could be very wet; you could perhaps find an aerial view of it on google-earth or similar. The Lairig Noe is quite high, but there seems to be a good track from there down to the road, from where it's "not far" to Dalmally and the start of Route 108.

Good luck!

Janet Clark   SHT Sub-editor.

The Scottish Rights of Way and Access Society 24 Annandale Street Edinburgh EH7 4AN (Registered Office)
Tel/Fax 0131 558 1222 e-mail: info@scotways.com web: www.scotways.com

Sunset over the eastern Ben Cruachan range

Back at my tent I had a look around the immediate vicinity and noticed that 'developments' of sorts were underway. I made good use of a nearby wooden picnic table and chairs that evening and for the following morning's breakfast. There were also new access gates being installed, new fenced off areas with curious looking mounds, sapling trees, an upturned wheelbarrow, white protective sheeting on the ground, and a sign proclaiming funding from 'The People's Postcode Lottery'. Someone must have got lucky…

I got talking to a man who was delivering stone aggregate to site, and he told me that this was the beginnings of Dalmally Community Orchard. All these years later it is great to see how (what has become) the 'Glenorchy and Innishail Community Orchard and Wild Woodland Garden' has developed, all the funders that have been involved and all the evident hard work that has gone into it. Quite clearly and in keeping with the rest of the Highlands, this community is doing far more than selling shortbread and pots of jam to passers-by. More information at loch-awe.com.

Quoting my diary: "Beautiful camp, beautiful evening, calm, cool and clear." I could not sum up the end of day twelve better myself. It was a stunner, even the campsite porridge was good.

Friday May 2, day 13 • Dalmally to Portsonachan

Dalmally

It was another very early start. 4am sounds ridiculous but the reality is that this far north, in a thin-skinned tent, with daylight appearing seemingly not long after darkness falls, your body rhythm does start to change. This combined with getting to sleep I guess around 9pm actually amounts to a good night.

Ben Cruachan

Carraig Gheal Wind Farm seen beyond the waters of Loch Awe

By the time June 21 comes about it hardly gets properly dark at all in these parts and especially so the further north you go. Nothing like the extremes of northern Scandinavia of course, but challenging nonetheless if you are not used to sleeping outside. My arrythmia was also a nuisance overnight and the inevitable need for a small-hours pee meant that trying to stay cocooned in the tent became a losing battle. Sometimes the best plan is to give up and get going. On this morning, when I did, I felt a whole lot better, it was as if my dicky ticker was just getting excited and wanted to get on with the journey.

The weather was breezy, sunny, dry, and cool; perfect for a short day's walk to my next stop; the unabashed luxury of my pre-arranged stay in the fleshpots of the four-star Portsonachan Hotel. This was my 'get past Ben Cruachan plan' and I was very much looking forward to it. I had booked not just B&B but B&B&B. Bed and Breakfast and Boat!

Today's walk was all on roads, part old military and part modern tarmac. From Dalmally I followed the road along Leac na Ceardaich out of the village towards the Donnchadh Bàn Mac an t-Saoir (Duncan Ban MacIntyre) Monument, built in honour of the renowned Scot's Gaelic poet. For reasons unknown I completely passed it by; I didn't even photograph it. Actually the reasons are completely obvious: I was wanting to get booked in to the hotel as soon as I could. At £100 for the night this was by far the most I had ever spent on an overnight stay anywhere, although admittedly the boat requirement was a bit of a one-off, so actually quite a bargain with that included, personal service n all. I was determined to get as much as possible out of my one night stay!

Once past the monument extensive views across Loch Awe started to open up, views which are best seen from the monument (so I am informed) for which it is famous, besides its literary connections. Looking south-west along the length of the sparkling waters of the loch and some ten miles distant I could see the turbines of the Carraig Gheal Wind Farm, rotating, glinting, and dancing in the breeze. To the northwest

the view is dominated by the massive bulk of Ben Cruachan with the dam which forms the Cruachan Reservoir clearly in view. All about is power; wind and water; the Highlands have all of these in abundance. If there is one reason that England needs Scotland to stay in the United Kingdom, it is this. My personal reason is very simple; I love Scotland and its people; being separated would not feel right.

Portsonachan Hotel and Loch Awe

149

Fresh milk!

Morning was not even half done when I arrived at the Portsonachan Hotel. I checked in immediately half expecting to be told to come back in the afternoon but to my astonishment my accommodation was ready. Second surprise was the type of accommodation; I mean a nice room overlooking the loch would have been more than adequate but a whole self-catering apartment was totally unexpected – and a balcony! I was handed the key shortly after 10am and all uncertainty about the booking had gone, even the all-essential boat was confirmed and arranged for the morning.

Four-star self-catering indulgence at the Portsonachan Hotel

I took full advantage of the facilities to get everything properly dry again; a backpacker's camping gear is rarely dry, most of the time it is in differing states of dampness; the main benefit of dry gear is keeping the weight of the rucksack down. Dampness in clothing and kit can add a surprising amount of additional weight. It was also good to be able to spread out the last two maps that Janine had sent to the hotel. The end was well in sight now. The rest of the day I spent wandering around the locality talking to the cows and generally appreciating the surroundings.

Portsonachan is a tiny place strung along the single track B840 road which hugs the south shore of Loch Awe for some 20 miles between Cladich and Ford at the south-western end of the loch and is mainly comprised of the hotel which seems to have swallowed up what few private cottages there were on the other side of the road. It has a pleasant feeling of isolation about it similar to taking the Corran Ferry to

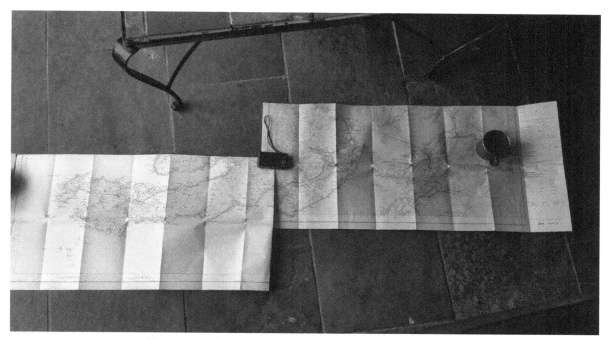

Time to spread out the maps and review the final part of the route

the opposite side of Loch Linnhe to Fort William at Camusnagaul, although at Portsonachan you are on the busier side of the water.

Finally it was time to get some food. No problems this evening. I sat down in the Cruachan `a la carte Restaurant and Bar feeling ever so slightly conspicuous, although I need not have felt that way as I had the place to myself. Maybe the residents knew something I was unaware of…

I looked at the food on the menu and soon determined that my usual order was all I wanted. Less than twenty minutes later I was regretting my decision. It was the worst fish and chips so far. By this stage of my walk and having consumed a dozen or so orders of said cuisine along the way, I reckoned I knew a thing or two about our most famous of dishes. The fish was bland the batter was damp, the chips the same. I ate half of it, drank the unnoteworthy beer, left the table and returned to my apartment. I hope the other guests made more imaginative choices from the menu; on reflection I should have done likewise. All a bit odd really; being right next to one of Scotland's biggest lochs, you would have thought 'fish' would have been a safe choice!

Portsonachan Hotel

Saturday May 3, day 14 ● Portsonachan to Loch Nell

The sun casts its sunrise spell on Loch Awe

After a delicious deep sleep dreaming of Kirkintilloch Fish Suppers in the sumptuous luxury of the hotel's bed, I was awake early again as if I were in the tent and not shielded from the early daylight. Fact was that the curtains held back and up against the roof window were even less effective than tent fabric at keeping the light out of the room; this added to the brightly decorated open-plan layout of the apartment was not conducive to sleep after sunrise; dawn dawned brightly and effectively.

Outside the bright start rapidly became overcast but only for a short time as blue skies returned again as I sat down for an early breakfast hoping and praying that last night's chef was on leave. In stark contrast to yesterday evening's droopingly disappointing fish n chips, breakfast was up to the standard you might expect in such an establishment. It was excellent. Also in contrast to twelve hours earlier the Cruachan à la carte Restaurant and Bar was busy with guests all chattering away enthusiastically about the day ahead.

I much prefer a bit of hustle, bustle, and noise to those 'whispers only' situations you sometimes get in a B&B where you dare not chink your spoon against your bowl, or worse crunch your cornflakes too loudly lest the silence be broken, and God forbid you to pass wind from any orifice. At least in a busy place you can release one and attempt to make out it was someone else. Have I just had Bill Bryson moment? (one of my favourite authors)

The third B of my deal at the Portsonachan Hotel

Successfully maintaining both composure and bodily function I got talking to a nice chap from Tonbridge in Kent who gave me £10 for Cre8. If memory serves me well by this stage of the walk I had raised nearly £2000 for Cre8 Macclesfield mainly resulting from local campaigning by family and friends, so it was good to receive the occasional freewill donation on route and to be able to talk about both my fundraising cause and the walk. Once again the 'are you on a pilgrimage' question was raised. In some ways the question can be a bit tiresome, but in another way it is good to know that people are alive to the formative history of our island.

I collected my gear together from the apartment and went to reception to pay my bill and report my displeasure with the evening meal. I do not like complaining but the food really was so poor I thought I would be doing an otherwise excellent hotel a disservice if I left and said nothing. Suffice to say the cost

of my meal (£30) was refunded with a profuse apology 'on behalf of the kitchen'. I had arranged for my personal ferry service across the loch to leave at 8.30am; so, duly satisfied with the hotel's guest services, I made my way down to the jetty and waited for my pilot who turned up bang on time. He was a quiet fella, who I assumed was on the staff of the hotel. As we crossed the loch it did occur to me that he might have been the chef that prepared my food, but I kept my counsel on the subject; both my safe passage and the successful conclusion of my walk in a timely manner depended on staying on good terms with him.

Crossing Loch Awe ~ looking back to the hotel and forward to Taycreggan

Crossing the calm waters of Loch Awe with the now blue skies overhead and the last leg of my second walk across mainland Scotland beckoning, I was quietly on a high and revelling in the fact that my plan for getting past Ben Cruachan had at last, after many months of waiting, actually come to pass. All I had to do now was get off the boat without falling in, which I managed on the second attempt, the first nearly got us both wet.

I shouted grateful thanks to the ferryman and walked up the grass on the jetty. He hollered and gestured back at me pointing at his dayglow lifejacket which had a striking resemblance to the one I was wearing. Red-faced I returned the swimming aid hoping that I would not need it during the rest of the walk.

Promising signs

It had taken all of ten minutes to cross the deep, cold blue waters of Loch Awe and presently I was soon climbing the road away from the lochside towards Kilchrenan, where one of the hardest parts of the entire route started; with a blocked footpath. I was stood in exactly the right place, as indicated on the map, where a footpath is clearly marked by the Ordnance Survey. I verified my position using GPS, but I could not see any sign of a path at the roadside or beyond. A little further on there were signs of another kind, but any notion of a path was still conspicuous by its absence. At the north end of Kilchrenan a signpost erected originally by the Scottish Rights of Way Society proclaims, "Public Footpath to Kilmore 11" and points vaguely at the rising grassland and also right at a hawthorn tree that was effectively blocking the way. Now I am usually pretty good at spotting the slightest indication of a footpath but search as I did, here there was nothing, not a clue. What followed was a battle across some of the hardest ground I have ever had the displeasure of negotiating; every walker's nightmare - big tough grass and heather tussocks. About two miles of them.

An unpromising start to the Midmuir Drove Road

All I could do was aim for the line of pylons on the skyline which was maddeningly difficult and punishing with a full rucksack on. I started shouting at every tussock, each one in my head taking on the proportions of Chewbacca and each having leg-twisting potential. I had to stop and calm down. It really was not that bad, but I was letting the fact that this was the first part of the entire route which was unexpectedly 'undefined' get to me. I am glad no-one other than my Creator saw me, I must have been an unedifying sight.

Sometimes I can totally forget my situation. Skies were virtually cloudless, the views towards Ben Cruachan were superb; conditions really were as benign as they could be, but I lost patience and very nearly missed all of it. Stopping was the best thing I could have done. Solo walking does have the odd down side; in this situation you need someone to tell you to get real and stop whinging, but in the absence of a companion you can become totally self-obsessed and lack any sense of objectiveness; this is never a good thing, especially in my case.

Once past the line of pylons I made a beeline towards the forest and at last found evidence that I was actually on the right route. Seeing a line and a positioning marker on a GPS device is one thing but seeing marks on the ground is far more assuring. It took me two hours to cover those three miles from Kilchrenan, my slowest progress yet, but upon reaching Loch Nant the 'Midmuir Drove Road' took on an altogether much more agreeable nature and my pace recovered back to normal. My troubles were behind me; for the time being.

Beyond the forest, much of which had been felled, and beyond the old sheilings of Midmuir at the western end of Sìor Loch, the landscape starts to take on a familiar appearance, very reminiscent of parts of the

The Ben Cruachan range rises beyond the Kilchrenan tussocky hinterland

Loch Nant

Peak District that lie within half-an-hour's drive of my home in Macclesfield. With Ben Cruachan now absent from the view and by the time I reached Creag Mhor where the metalled road is joined, I could be forgiven for thinking I was somewhere near Buxton, with hills of modest proportions on all sides and the occasional hilltop draped over with a cloak of commercial forest.

Signs of a track appear albeit for four wheels rather than four hooves

An old Scottish Rights of Way Society double-headed arrow sign was a timely reminder of where I was and further evidence of just how long this organisation had been working to improve accessibility across Scotland.

Like many niche organisations Scotways has a small core of staff supported by an army of dedicated but sparsely distributed volunteers. In locations like this with such a huge geographical area to cover, you realise just how gargantuan their task is, and how lucky those of us south of the border are to have such a well-developed network of footpaths, clearly marked on maps both online and offline, but most importantly and in most cases, marked by signposting literally at every path entrance, no matter how small and insignificant they may be. England is peculiar. As anyone resident in or familiar with the USA will tell you, the idea that the general public can have a right of way across your land, protected in Law, is beyond contemplation.

I enjoyed the last few miles of easy road walking into Kilmore, the nightmare of the first few miles from Kilchrenan already feeling like yesterday and no longer of significance.

Peak District-like landscapes at the head of Glen Feochan

It was late afternoon by the time I arrived at Loch Nell, my planned location for the night. I found a suitable patch of grass on the lochside, put up my tent and then realised that I had run out of water. Rather than use nearby sources with all the inherent sheep-related risks that involves, I walked back to the house I had passed, alongside the entrance to a few traditionally styled self-catering cottages, and knocked on the door. Mary MacKinnon, proprietor of 'Clan Cottages' answered, and could not have been more helpful. Not only did she give me all the water I needed but she also gave me a small bottle of Grant's whisky and a packet of shortbread. Best of all she brewed up for me and suggested I move my tent from the lochside and into her secure sheep-free garden (albeit guarded by a large cockerel).

Wishing I had called at the house before pitching camp, I scurried back to the lochside and dismantled my tent not paying any of my usual attention to how well it was packed. My friend hindsight tells me I should have left the pole in place, removed the pegs, and just picked the whole thing up! Within 20 minutes it was re-erected in Mary's garden. I quickly felt at home and looked forward to what I hoped was going to be another good but brief night in my nylon home. I was just in time; at 5.30pm it started raining. Unbeknown to me at the time it was to continue raining for most of my walk across Mull.

As with camp 8 at Dalmally, camp 9 also had two versions; it seems I was pining for upgrades all the time, although I did take a cabin downgrade at Inverarnan, so fairs fair!

Mary said she was going into Oban and asked if I wanted anything. At first I said no thank you, but as she was getting into her car I changed my mind and asked for a pint of milk. Why does my brain never work when I need it to? Mary was very welcoming and really hospitable. I have absolutely no doubt that the MacKinnons are great hosts for their holiday makers. More information at clancottages.com.

Camp 9 versions 1 & 2 ~ the latter included whisky, tea and shortbread 😊

Sunday May 4, day 15 ● Loch Nell to Oban

Cockerels are annoyingly reliable; and as if it were necessary to prove this fact he delivered his first fanfare at precisely 4am. Quickly reminding myself of the benefits gained a few hours earlier I buried my head in my sleeping bag (making no difference whatsoever to the penetrating cock-a-doodle-dos) and gained a degree of slumber for about forty minutes by which time all the other locals, both winged and hoofed, were joining in to proclaim the start of the day. From a nature-loving perspective I should of course have welcomed all of this, but on this particular morning I was not quite as 'connected' as I should have been. By 5am I gave in, fired up the JetBoil and made porridge.

Despite occasional rain overnight the weather was noticeably milder, in fact warm to the point that up to when my feathered friend made his presence known my sleeping bag was off my shoulders for the first time. Also of note was that when I dozed off in a whisky fuelled haze at about 8.30pm it was windy but as I woke up all was calm with hardly a breath of wind. Change was in the air.

Today was notable for three reasons; firstly because all being well I was to complete my second walk across Scotland, next because I would have to use a ferry for the second time (albeit substantively larger

Loch Nell

than the first) and lastly because I would step on the third island of my walk; the first being Lindisfarne and the second being Great Britain; the fourth would be Iona. With these thoughts in mind I struck camp, this time packing the tent away with my usual level of care and attention, shouldered the rucksack and set off towards the busiest and most popular place of my entire route: Oban.

Walking along the road away from Loch Nell out of necessity my thoughts were turning towards the Isle of Mull and Iona; necessary because I was being overcome with premature feelings of walk completion. With just over 40 miles to go this was no time to be thinking about the journey home, there was another island to cross including the wildest wettest camp I have ever endured.

Calm and mercifully dry conditions continued as I turned off the road, bidding a fond hope-to-see-you-again farewell to Loch Nell and Mary, and walked around Cnoc Mòr into the forest following the track past Lochan Eilean towards Glencruitten House where, somewhere in its vicinity between Black Mount and the road, I encountered the strange individuals seen in these pictures. Janine said one of them had an uncanny resemblance of someone she knew. I have absolutely no idea what she was on about.

Wooden watchers

As I entered the outskirts of Oban it started. I mean it properly started. It was like passing through a curtain as if entering a whole new watery world. Down at the ferry terminal it was already starting to get busy even at the early hour of 8.20am on a Sunday morning, but I was pleased to join the modest throng of passengers and gratefully entered the large heated and air-conditioned waiting area to shelter and become less wet. I had not been this soaked through since leaving Lindisfarne. The water was starting to find weaknesses in my 'clever-tech' defences.

Oban ~ CalMac land!

Caledonian MacBrayne ferries are today more synonymous to the Western Isles of Scotland than British Rail was to Britain's railways and has stood the test of time, still being wholly owned by the Scottish Government. Long may it remain so. The very idea of this stalwart of public transport services being handed over to the private sector for 'efficiency savings' and 'rebranding' fills me with horror. 'CalMac' are part of the fabric of the Western Isles economy, and for the majority critical to their lifeblood. Apart from anything else the ferries look superb, somehow they just look right, they fit the scene. Private sector …keep yer thieving hands off!

The ferry MV Isle of Mull departed the Oban terminal at 9.50am on the dot and for a short while longer my shelter from the rain continued as I boarded hermetically sealed from the elements in an air bridge

Oban

similar to that commonly used in airports. My second solo walk across Great Britain was completed; now it was time for the final lap across Mull to commence but not in this part of the book, I will continue my recollections in part seven. Seems like the right thing to do even if it is part way through a day…

Leaving Oban behind ~ Goodbye Great Britain ~ for now

PART SEVEN

Mull

Craignure to Fionnphort

Sunday May 4, day 15 • Craignure to Glenbyre

Craignure (just to confirm)

Craignure's bustling shopping centre

I almost regretted the respite and false sense of security gained on the ferry crossing, as all too soon and just as I was getting comfortable the ferry arrived at Craignure's terminal quay; it was time to face another soaking. Honestly, I am treating rain like some sort of enemy, like something alien and not rightly 'of this world'. I look well going on about the glory of Creation and then complaining about precipitation - one of its greatest design successes! Part of being human I guess; 'familiarity breeds contempt' did someone once say?

Opposite the ferry terminal Craignure stretches along one side of the main road that serves the Isle of Mull. Most traffic heads north-west via Salen to Tobermory of fine single malt and Ballamory fame, the rest briefly head south to Lochdon where the road then turns west towards Fionnphort and Iona, passing through Bunessan on the way. In the absence of any defined footpaths in the area my planned walking route was to follow the road to Loch Spelve turning on to the minor road at Strathcoil in the hope of finding a suitable spot for a wild camp somewhere on the shoreline. I called in the Spar shop to stock up on supplies and also bought a copy of the West Highland Free Press. On the way out of the shop I couldn't help noticing the yucca type plants standing tall in front of the terraced house next door. Evidently it does not always rain and perhaps because of being so sheltered from the west Craignure must also enjoy a generally mild climate. I will not go so far as to say 'semi-tropical'.

Rain rain glorious rain

Shouldering my rucksack, I started walking, or should I say splashing, towards Lochdon. As always, once I got going, I was fine. As Billy Connolly famously once said "there's no such thing as bad weather, just the wrong clothing", which is why here I will take this opportunity to comment on **modern rainwear…**

Wainwright famously never possessed any, much preferring a more traditional tweed coat or overcoat. In my case, I have on a few occasions now, misplaced my faith in garments made with one of those well-known 'clever-tech' type microporous fabrics, and have spent more than a few hundreds of pounds on what are supposed to be waterproof jackets made with it. They have all, without exception, not met expectations. It is not that they have not worked at all, they just have not worked for very long. In my experience any waterproof qualities that they have are quickly lost, usually within a couple of days walking in continuous rain. I have had jackets replaced, I have used recommended washing methods using expensive soaps and waterproofers that the manufacturers specify. I have 'air-dried', low-temperature tumble dried; I have done it all, but all to no avail. After a day like today I always end up with a very damp fleece jacket and/or shirt and/or vest. Once these high-priced so-called waterproofs lose that intial duck's-back beading ability to shed water it never, but never, returns. 'Clever-tech' fabrics as I call them are not only meant to defend the wearer from rain on the outside, but also facilitate the venting of dampness from within caused by perspiration. Great theory. I think Wainwright may have got wet through on occasion, but at least he could rest in the knowledge that he did not part with hundreds of pounds in the process. Sometimes I think a 'Last of the Summer Wine' Cleggy style pack-a-mac costing a couple of quid would be better value. I exaggerate, but you know what I mean.

On a totally unrelated subject I have just spent nearly an hour trying to locate this postbox. All the way through this book I have tried to select photographs that I can be reasonably confident of being able to locate for the sake of the description below each where appropriate. Most are easy and obvious but there have been exceptions where a fair degree of head-scratching has been involved. The picture you see to the left is a classic case in point…

Time for a technical interlude!

Digital photography has a few advantages over methods of image capture from the pre-computer age, one of them being that each picture has a time stamp listed in the file properties. Those in the know will when necessary be used to right-clicking the image file and finding the date and time taken information listed in the details tab of the resulting dialogue (sorry for getting a bit techy here, it was bound to happen sometime). Doing computer technology support for a day job for twenty years I am, supposedly, counted amongst 'those in the know', but on this occasion I got lazy because in modern Windows operating systems you can also see the date/time taken information by hovering your mouse pointer over the image in your picture libraries.

That is where the trouble started, because for reasons best known to Microsoft, the lazy method does not always work, and you are instead presented with a time record which can differ substantively from the aforementioned details. On this occasion Mr Foolish here totally forgot this apparent anomaly and trusted the lazy information, which suggested that I had taken all of three-and-a-half hours to walk from Craignure to this postbox, whose location I *thought* was near Torosay. Something was clearly wrong. Was I crawling? Had I shacked up in the pub and belatedly given up on the whole idea of walking to Iona? Where was I?!

Therefore, in the interest of diligent book research, I have searched all the likely places on Google StreetView ably assisted by postboxes.dracos.co.uk (which is a particularly useful postbox locator service; sort of thing you need in 2021) concentrating on the few road junctions between Kinlochspelve and Lochbuie. At my usual rain-fuelled walking pace of around 3mph that is the area I should have been, at least ten miles along the road from Craignure. I found other postboxes, all built into the local vernacular arch-topped brick pillar, but not *this* postbox. Of course, eventually my technical light bulb switched on and I checked the details properly showing a time difference of just half-an-hour between the picture of the Spar shop in Craignure and the location of the postbox shown in the picture, which I am relieved to confirm, is on the road near Torosay Castle. My memory serves me reasonably well, I am not so sure about my computer.

I could of course have just not included the picture of the postbox, but then you would never have known where it is, and neither would you have discovered that fab postbox locator service, so no complaining! Anyway, I once read in a book about landscape photography that British and presumably Scottish landscapes are always enhanced by a splash of red, so on that basis the picture stays. Read on!

Loch Uisg near Uamh nam Misichean 'Cave of the Misses'

HM Queen Victoria's diamond jubilee cairn

A wet rucksack is a heavy rucksack

Lochbuie Post Office

Honesty shop

BUSINESS HOURS

OPEN Most Days About 9 or 10
Occasionally as Early as 7, But SOME DAYS
As Late As 12 or 1.
WE CLOSE About 5:30 or 6
Occasionally About 4 or 5, But
Sometimes as Late as 11 or 12.
SOME DAYS OR Afternoons, We
Aren't Here At All, and Lately
I've Been Here Just About All The Time,
Except When I'm Someplace Else,
But I Should Be Here Then, Too.

By the time I had walked to Loch Spelve I was not ready for stopping as planned, especially in the rain which continued unabated. I also realised that I could not possibly get any wetter than I already was, so I continued past Loch Uisg and the surprisingly located memorial cairn commemorating Her Majesty Queen Victoria`s Diamond Jubilee (22 June 1897), to the Post Office at Lochbuie; the first shelter since disembarking the ferry. Gratefully I stepped inside and dropped my rucksack to the floor where it was quickly surrounded by a pool of water.

Lochbuie Post Office is not only unusual because of its diminutive size but also because it provides an 'honesty shop' where you can make your own brew, buy a cake or two or even a souvenir. I skipped the latter offer but invested heavily in the former. Never before was a cup of tea better located and absolutely no confusion about my time of arrival; I was there at exactly 3.30pm.

This was another of those strange days when you feel as though you are in a time-warp, and in part is the reason that I decided to split this day between part six and seven of this book, so serving to emphasise the point. After putting due payment in the honesty box, I left the Post Office and walked beyond the end of the tarmac road following the track towards Carsaig noting the increasingly wild nature of the south Mull coast. Loch Nell and Mary's kind hospitality seemed an age away even though I was there only yesterday. The ferry and the rain seemed to act as remarkably effective time shifters, I felt as though I had passed through a time warp somewhere on the Sound of Mull.

Beyond the buildings at Glenbyre where the broken line on the map easily skips across the Glenbyre Burn without reference to a bridge but instead indicating the presence of stepping stones. There is (or was) in fact a footbridge or at least the remains of one... To an 'adrenaline junkie' I am sure that this

Glenbyre Burn footbridge as it was on Sunday 4 May 2014

modest little bridge would be of no consequence, but for me with heavy wet sack on shoulders, it was enough to cause hestitation. If I were unlucky, and it chose to break just at the moment I happened to use it, I suppose the worst that could have happened would have been a full soaking and maybe a bruise or two and a dented pride. As a solo walker this was definitely an outcome to be avoided at an age when a broken bone is also a distinct possibility.

I opened the gate and stepped gingerly onto the soaked timbers crossing with four or five carefully aimed steps to the other side. Hopefully all these years later the bridge has been repaired. Once across I walked down towards the sea where I laughed as I realised that I could have crossed the burn barefoot where it spreads wide across the shingle beach with a fraction of the risk. You live and learn.

Glenbyre Burn crosses the shingle beach

About a few hundred yards beyond the Glenbyre Burn I found one of the very few patches of grass hereabouts suitable for pitching a tent at grid reference NM 581230 in the shadow of steep cliffs just below a cave marked on the map near Uaimh nan Tàillearan. To this day this is easily the wildest place I have ever camped. With numerous waterfalls pouring off the hills fuelled by unremitting heavy rain, and

Spot the tent! Camp 10 near Uaimh nan Tàillearan (apologies for the pic quality ~ very little light)

with the sea angrily chewing at the seaward end of Loch Buie under a heavy grey sky, I fully expected to see a man-eating dinosaur appear around the headland. This was a scene from The Lost World!

Darkness was creeping over both sea and land as I spilled a very wet tent on to the sodden grass and assembled the single pole which pinged into shape without encouragement. Pushing it into the wet fly sheet sleeve was a different order of challenge and pinning the tent to the ground was another as it was wildly caught like a sail by the brisk onshore wind. Once again though my excellent Terra Nova tent soon stabilised and became a very essential shelter from the tumult all around; this was a real tent test, one that despite its nine years, it passed with flying colours.

For twenty minutes or so I stood in the rain in the forlorn hope that the inner tent might become a little less wet and then spread my emergency Sol bivvy bag on the floor with my excellent Thermarest sleep mat on top. I ducked inside as carefully as possible, stripping off my supposed-to-be waterproof jacket on the way in, disposing of it in the small porch along with my rucksack. Once inside I replaced damp shirt and trousers with PJs, shoved my legs into my sleeping bag and donned my duck down jacket which, if kept dry, provides all the warmth I need.

Manoeuvring in the confines of a small one-man tent is a challenge at the best of times but doing this at the same time as trying not to touch the sides thereby distributing damp makes it doubly interesting. Anyone looking on would no doubt have enjoyed the spectacle. Adding to the entertainment I fired up the JetBoil which with a woosh and loud 'poof' excitedly exploded into life. I cooked some pasta, made a brew, and lived to tell the tale. My JetBoil friend can be a bit lively at times, but it has never harmed me, well not yet anyway. Another excellent piece of kit.

Finally, I cocooned myself and managed a couple of hours sleep. Heavy rain continued unabated but eventually the wind lessened allowing me to hear the sea and nearby waterfalls. My little world was alive with water on all sides and conducive to sleeping but there was a side-effect to which I eventually had to submit by venturing outside in the rain, in my birthday suit, to answer both numbers from an urgent call of nature. Eventually sounds of ocean and waterfalls merged and as the wind breathed its last I started to hear owls calling from the cliffs. No dinosaurs tonight. I felt closer to nature than at any other time in my life and was humbled and thankful as a result. Memories are made of this.

View south-east from camp 10 across Loch Buie to Rubha na Faoilinn

Monday May 5, day 16 • Glenbyre to Camas

Camp 10 ~ the morning after

Waking again a couple of hours later at around 4am I knew I could not get back to sleep. Amazingly I was too warm in a tent that only five or six hours previously was as wet inside as out and was now reasonably dry. I must have been generating a lot of heat! To busy myself I started sorting out the chaos of my confined world and in the process discovered a sorry looking GPS device. Damp had penetrated the device through its USB socket (rubber bung was missing and was substituted with Blu-Tack) and was manifesting in the form of condensation on the screen. I knew this was potentially serious and therefore did not switch it on. Instead I wrapped it up in my copy of the West Highland Free Press bought in Craignure; hoping that it would absorb the moisture which, as I discovered later, had found its way onto the motherboard. I was glad that I had my paper maps as backup; the sat-naff had succumbed to the rain and was no more, not even the pages of the West Highland Free Press could save it.

Having mentioned the West Highland Free Press three and now four times I thought I should explain what it is. As you probably have already guessed it is a local newspaper, but it is one that I have known for a very long time. Janine and I used to subscribe to it back in the eighties when we were actively seeking work on Skye with a view to living there, so for a time we were very much in tune with local issues of the day, foremost of which was the debate around tolls associated with the proposed bridge linking Skye and the mainland at the Kyle of Lochalsh. Founded in 1972 today this superb independent newspaper is wholly owned by its employees and has a circulation across all of the West Highlands and Islands and beyond. More information at whfp.com.

Having got the tent interior into some sort of order and having consigned the GPS to the bottom of my rucksack for the journey home, I set about writing a section in my notebook to address the pilgrimage question which I reckoned on possibly having to answer again towards the end of the walk. I must have concluded that the best way to clarify the answer in my own head was to write it down, so I spent an hour doing just that. Rather than reproduce it in typescript here I thought I should add a little authenticity by photographing the pages which are shown in the final part of this book.

That done by 5:15am it was time for breakfast. My notebook is diligent on the question of pilgrimage but makes no reference whatsoever to what I had for breakfast that morning other than I had one; it was probably the usual porridge maybe with some nuts and raisins thrown in to add interest. Two weeks in my culinary excesses tend to lose their appeal but needs must.

By 6.30am I was washed up with tent packed away, and on the path heading west, feeling at last in control of my circumstances. I continued the walk along the coast to Carsaig which was only about two-an-a-half miles from where I was camped to the road end. It seemed twice as far. The rain mercifully kept at bay and the tide was out, so I was able to dodge as many rocky obstacles as possible towards the water's edge, but the going was still tough for what is an established coastal path. Perhaps I was missing the path by being too far down the beach, that is also possible.

Numerous caves and waterfalls punctuate the basalt cliffs hereabouts making this walk rewarding in spectacular measure. In one or two places you can see rock formations similar to those seen at Fingal's Cave on the Isle of Staffa to the north of Iona and on Northern Ireland's Giant's Causeway. Every corner you turn is a photographer's paradise, even the goats are photogenic. Out at sea there are seals, dolphins, whales, and basking sharks to be seen, Golden Eagles circle overhead. The only species that you might expect to see I did not come across anywhere between Lochbuie and Carsaig; humans were completely absent. Given the goings on around my tent that night, that was probably a good thing.

Cliffs and goats watch every move I make between camp 10 and Carsaig

It was with some relief I reached the road end at Carsaig. It had been quite an adventure, especially for a town lad like me, and one that I will never forget. This was my first proper acquaintance with wild Mull, and I was captivated.

Actually, this was my second encounter but the first one I would rather forget. On that occasion as a green twenty-something, I was camped at the foot of Ben More in August somewhere in Gleann Dubh above Ardvergnish. It was a long time ago on one of my first solo expeditions to the islands in the days before I had learned respect for the local wildlife in the form of those tiniest of foes; the Highland midge *Culicoides impunctatus*. It was a warm, still sultry morning and foolishly I had camped by a stream. To cut a long story short I ended up sat in the stream up to my neck in water to eat my cornflakes. The midges had their fill of me that morning; they showed no mercy. I vowed to never again wild camp in August north of the border and to this day I plan all walks in Scotland so that they are well done before June.

Carsaig Bay

Carsaig ~ the beautiful roadside waterfall of Eas na Dabhaich ~ remember what I said about a splash of red?

The road north across the Ross of Mull

'Impunctatus' is an exceptionally good name for them as they puncture skin, particularly white English sassenach skin, very effectively. What they lack in size they make up for in merciless blood sucking hordes. Ignore them at your peril! These are true Highlanders!

Following the road and climbing steeply up and away from Carsaig, and as I started the four-mile crossing of the Ross of Mull north to Pennyghael, rain started to fall again with renewed vigour. My suspicions that the relatively dry conditions of the morning so far were respite only from the rain that

The main road west hugs the northern shoreline of the Ross of Mull

had been falling most of the time since Oban, were confirmed. It was going to be another wet one but at least this time the day would not end under ripstop nylon but hopefully under a solid slate roof instead. In my original itinerary a lochside camp was planned at Pennyghael but arriving here as I was at 9.30am

Getting nearer

I was way too early, all consequential of yesterday's marathon effort and walking eight miles further than planned to Glenbyre. Ah well, plans are plans said the minister.

I was soon walking along Mull's main road and heading west on the last few miles of the journey. In the misty distance the hills of Iona were in sight. Journey's end was near, but the day was far from done. All road-walking now, no more route finding, the GPS could rest in peace deep in its WHFP newspaper cocoon, this was one of those days when you just trudge, one foot in front of the other, left right left right left right, splashing through as many puddles as possible for entertainment. Next stop Camas – so I thought.

Approaching Bunessan I am having another of those moments when recollections are proving tricky, but my black police-book notes are, as always, a valuable way of jogging the grey matter. Memories are vague but I recall making prior arrangement to meet the South Mull Ranger, at the Ross of Mull Historical

View across Loch na Corrobha and Loch Scridain towards
the primeval terraced headland of Bearraich on the Ardmeanach peninsula

Nearer still!

Centre in Bunessan, with the intention of us trying a new off-road route that was being explored as an alternative for walkers, but for tomorrow, not today. I pressed on anyway fully intending to ignore the time difference and just turn up. I could at the very least have a look around and say hello.

At about 2.30pm and after some 13 miles of road walking from Carsaig I arrived in Bunessan and wasted no time in seeking shelter from the incessant rain by finding the aforementioned visitor centre at Millbrae Cottage which, as I went in, seemed unstaffed. Once again, substantial puddles formed around me as I lowered my sodden rucksack onto the tiled floor.

Roadside brew

Moments like this remind me of my first job in early eighties, when I used to motorcycle each day to the offices of Hartington Fleming and Worsley Architects near Altrincham from Bramhall. On wet days I was ordered to drip dry before entering, and still get to my drawing board on time. Or else!

Millbrae Cottage ~ home to the Ross of Mull Historical Centre (2013 picture kindly supplied by ROMHC)

Having regained my composure after fighting my way out of my not-waterproofs, I started browsing the few exhibits around the well-organised walls when Emily Wilkins, the impressively titled 'South Mull, Iona, Staffa, and Burg Ranger' appeared. Emily quickly and very kindly made me a brew having remembered our conversation and the arrangement we had made. Being a day early Emily was understandably otherwise engaged so we could not walk as planned, but she did spend time asking me about my walk. It was good to talk; and at the very least it was a chance to shelter from the rain for half-an-hour or so.

As I was finishing my brew and towards the end of our conversation, Emily told me that a community café was being held in the local village hall until 4pm. I checked my watch, hurriedly changed my socks for drier versions, got the wet gear back on, shouldered my rucksack, thanked her for her hospitality, and got on my way. I did not want to miss out on the chance of soup, cakes, and more tea! More information about the Ross of Mull Historical Centre at romhc.org.uk. and the Mull ranger service at mict.co.uk/ranger-service.

On the road to Bunessan ~ Sometimes I am just unlucky!

At a personal record-breaking pace, I walked swiftly and determinedly to Bunessan Community Centre hoping not to be disappointed. I was only just in time as I walked into the hall at about 3.30pm. To my horror the local ladies and gent were packing away the tables, folding the legs as I arrived. "What's going

Bunessan Community Centre

on!?" I bawled at them. Only joking. Any such behaviour could potentially have earned me a swift and deserved exit head first into the loch! I chose a more diplomatic approach and asked if they were still open, all the time trying not to look at my watch…

I could not have been made more welcome as a table was hurriedly put back on its legs and a chair put in place, and shortly afterwards I was served a fabulous bowl of soup with a cheese and ham toastie followed by cakes and tea; all for £6. They were all proper angels. As they carried on packing away the bunting I was parried with questions about my walk, genuinely showing interest in my journey.

With spirits lifted and appetite satisfied I was ready for the last few miles to Camas which was a mile or so off route. Directly I had less than six miles walk to this journey's end.

Outside the road still glistened wet with rain although chinks in the cloud's armour were appearing. I dared to believe that the weather might brighten up for tomorrow and be kind to me on Iona. I was kid giddy with excitement.

Camas is an unusual outdoor activity centre run by the Iona Community. Really it is more of an outdoor 'experience' centre which, for many years, has hosted groups of disadvantaged youngsters from Macclesfield in the care of Cre8, and from similar organisations across the land. I was invited to stay for a night and see the place for myself having heard much about it. The 200-year-old renovated cottages are indicated as a 'fishing station (dis)' on OS maps ('dis' meaning disused) and ordinarily are inaccessible by road, the only access being by either boat or on foot down a one-and-a-half-mile track or 'driveway' as I refer to it in the pictures. Camas exists totally 'off-grid' and is largely self-sustaining being powered completely by renewable, mainly wind, energy. For young people

The end is nigh?

from the digital age many of whom are from broken households it is a transforming experience, benefitting the vast majority who go. Changed lives for the better are the result.

Camas has a very long 'driveway'...

...which you reach the end of ~ eventually

I arrived at about 5pm and was shown to my dormitory room which was a lot more basic than I expected; in fact, it was cold and uninviting with a bare dark floor and whitewashed stone walls, and of course no electric light. I did not like it at all and felt oddly unthankful for it. It was a really strange experience. What was I expecting? VIP treatment? Maybe a four-star hotel room? Whatever it was my reaction really took me by surprise and up until today, as I type this some seven years later, reasons are still unclear, other than to accept that my life generally is perhaps too comfortable making my expectations at the time unrealistic. Now, with time elapsed, I think I know why I reacted as I did; the story goes back a long way…

As a child and into my adolescence and early adulthood I was a bed wetter, and as a result, during my secondary school years, I was terrified at the prospect of staying in accommodation similar to the dorms at Camas in case the worst happened. Memories of trips to Malham and such places as part of secondary school geography field studies, and Sunday-school weekends away, are as potent as any I have of this walking journey. The curious thing was that when I was at Camas these memories did not surface, all I knew was that I did not want to be in that room.

I am fortunate to have been the child of loving parents, who helped and encouraged me as best as they could, despite the horrendous amount of work that I caused, particularly for my Mum. They never punished me for my mishaps, as I imagine would sometimes happen to children of my generation with similar developmental problems. Many of the young people who visit Camas do not have the benefits I

Camas

Bare essentials!

enjoyed of love and care at home. That is why I know the work of Cre8 and places like Camas are so vitally important. I therefore have no shame in sharing my story here to emphasise my personal appreciation of the ongoing work of Cre8, the Iona Community, Camas, and many similar organisations. Camas and its surroundings are scenically beautiful of that you can be sure, but the beauty is not just skin-deep, superficiality ends at the top of that long 'driveway'.

Having spread all of my gear including tent across the spare bunks in the dormitory to dry out I had a salad tea at 6.30pm mainly eating produce which was grown on site, all was good. The conversation ebbed and flowed in the dimly lit room, but I still felt like an outsider. John and the other staff that were at Camas at the time of my visit made me very welcome but despite all of their evident kindness my feelings of unease persisted. Of all the places you might have expected me to fit into like hand in glove, Camas would surely have been one of those places, but it was not to be. I have tried Youth Hostels on a number of occasions in the past and similar feelings persisted; all connected with my childhood.

Camas used to be a fishing community on the north Ross of Mull shoreline at Camas Tuath (bay)

I hope I have not painted a negative picture of Camas because that is not my intention. This was just me and my experience. Camas is brilliant in every way!

Tuesday May 6, day 17 ● Camas to Fionnphort

Was it my body clock or was it the cold? Whatever the cause I was awake at the first light of dawn; my watch said it was 4.30am. Maybe it was anticipation of the day ahead and the mixed feelings that the end of any long walk brings.

Breakfast was available to me from around 8am but with hours to wait and with eagerness to get going I decided instead to fire up the JetBoil, which roared into life with its usual jet engine reheat vibe. After a camp breakfast on the bare floor of the dorm I packed the semi-dry gear back into my rucksack and crept

The Camas 'driveway' ~ in reality a footway :)

out of the building in the hope of not disturbing anyone, either directly or with the assistance of any winged or legged creature that might be lurking around the cottages. My quiet exit was successful, but my progress came to a shuddering halt when a couple of hundred yards along the path a short intense shower doused me all over (like they do) as if my relatively dry condition needed rectifying and reverting back to type again, as if being less than properly wet all over was some sort of afront to the environment. I had set out with my down jacket on having worn it all night to insulate me from the cold of the dormitory; so now with much fumbling and a worrying spate of dad dancing I hurriedly donned my not-waterproof jacket (well it was better than nothing) in the hope of keeping the duck feathers dry. Morning drizzle continued as I walked back along the Camas footway towards the road and turned right for the ferry. I have concluded that 'driveway' is an unsuitable description.

As I faced west once again the skies cleared, the rain stopped, and grey clouds gave way to blue skies. At last! The brilliance of the sun after two days of dreich dullness was unforgettable. The sky cut apart and suddenly the colours of the landscape came alive. It was a really special moment; with only two miles to walk to the ferry I was full of excited anticipation, surely the walk could not end in a better way. After all the mixed

emotions, feelings and experiences of the last twenty-four hours, clouds were clearing my mind as well as the sky. For the first time since walking through the rain-veil into Oban, I actually started to feel dry; the warmth of the sun was intoxicating.

Even nearer!

The mysteriously named Loch Poit na h-I

Being as I was some 35 miles to the west; Oban felt a long way away; but then I remembered that in less than 48 hours I would back there again waiting for a train south to Glasgow and the foreign land beyond called England. Home was beckoning but first I had a ferry to catch which, predictably, I was much too early for. It was 7.40am when I walked into the small waiting room at the tiny Fionnphort ferry terminal. I checked the timetable; first crossing to Iona was just over an hour later so I was able to relax. It was good to have the timetable imposed on me, I was far too eager to get across to Iona which seemed close

St Ernan's Church overlooking Loch Poit na h-I

by and strangely far away at the same time. Across the stippled waters of the Sound of Iona the Abbey buildings were prominently in view as were all the habitations of Baile Mòr, which together form the island's sole village community; but for the nearby church I think it would more properly be described as a hamlet.

There was something very satisfying about seeing the end of my journey but not being quite there; in fact, I was very content

Arrival in Fionnphort ~ time to slow down!

enjoying the view of shifting skies and sea plus the anticipation of an imminent arrival at journey's end just half-a-mile away, so much so that I let the first ferry come and go, deciding to get on board the next. Leaving my rucksack in the still empty waiting room I walked down to the top of the slipway from where it was great to see the familiar livery of CalMac's 'Loch Buie' ro-ro ferry crossing the waters towards me in a great sweeping arc, semi-sideways crab-walk style. The pilot, or should I say captain, of the ferry told me that the Sound of Iona has currents second only in strength to the famous Coire Bhreacain (in English the Gulf of Corryvreckan) some 30 miles to the south-east of Iona between the isles of Jura and Scarba, where large whirlpools can capsize craft if in the hands of inexperienced or individuals disrespectful of nature's power; a mercifully rare occurrence. Definitely not a place for so-called adrenaline-junkies. Suffice to say MV Loch Buie needs experienced hands to make the regular daily crossings in all weathers.

The Abbey seen across the Sound of Iona

As mentioned before, finishing a long walk always delivers a stir of different emotions. On the one hand there is the simple feeling of achievement in completing what you set out to do, on the other there is the realisation that life generally fails to excite the senses in the way that a long walk does with all the different places that you see each day, the ever-changing weather, and the characters you meet along the way. When out on a long walk I sometimes crave the comforts of home, when at home I crave the trail and itch to be walking again. I have to admit; I am a restless soul!

Eager to be contactable I parked myself on one of the bench seats in the waiting room and plugged my phone into a socket conveniently located underneath. Dave and Janet were at some point in the next few hours likely to be in touch, so I was anxious not to have a dead phone. The GPS device was a different matter; I unwrapped it from the now damp newspaper and concluded that despite my best-efforts moisture had indeed got onto the device's motherboard. I tried powering it up, but it was totally dead. Did I mention that it was on loan to me? I messaged my friend Richard the owner to let him know at the same time promising to pay for its repair.

By the time I had done messaging various people about my whereabouts the ferry had returned and was being boarded for the second crossing of the day. I hauled on my rucksack and walked slowly down the ramp on to the third boat of my journey. At 10.10am I set foot on my fourth island. My walk from Lindisfarne to Iona was complete although I still had overnight accommodation to find.

Well, what more can I say? Plenty as it happens, but as you can see the title of this part is 'Mull' so the finale on Iona is coming up in part eight. You might have noticed a smudge in the top-right-hand-corner of some the pictures in these last few pages for which I apologise; at least you can be sure they are authentic as taken by this author and his greasy little fingers. Yes, I know it is only mid-morning, but rules are rules, the rest of this day is on another island. As with the Isle of Mull, Iona deserves its own part and that's that...

MV 'Loch Buie' makes the first crossing of the day from Fionnphort to Iona

PART EIGHT

Iona

Finale!

Tuesday May 6, day 17 • Iona

Final one of the walk

It is only a short walk from the ferry to the Abbey but despite this, and rather worryingly, I had actually plotted a route for the sat-nav; one as it turns out that I was never able to use, but nevertheless plot one I did. Was this yet another indication of OCD (Obsessive Compulsive Disorder – at this late stage in the book one must not presume upon anyone's knowledge of acronyms) and my apparent need to micromanage every step of the way? Well as it happens, no. It was just for the sake of completeness and an accurate count on the total mileage, which, including diversions to off-route accommodation and en-route 'corrections', I reckon was about 300 miles as I stepped through the doorway of St Oran's Chapel at the official end of my walk. It was about 10.30am.

On the way and on request I had the photo seen on final page 202 taken outside the Post Office by a couple of passers-by. Why the Post Office I hear you ask? Well not only because is it one of the country's most scenically located, but also because the familiar sign outside confirms my location. Actually there is a third reason: the roof was rebuilt by Cre8; not a bad place to learn roofing skills although best done without an Atlantic gale blowing as is common in these parts.

St Oran's Chapel

St Oran's Chapel

St Oran's is a very simple place of worship. Much like St Mary's on Lindisfarne they both are in the shadow of larger and better-known neighbouring buildings. Both are good places to stop, breathe, be silent and listen; the noisiest thing I was aware of was my heartbeat. Like St Aidan in 634AD who journeyed in the opposite direction, God had helped me all the way albeit in very different times and I imagine in starkly differing ways. I gave quiet thanks.

After twenty minutes or so I shouldered my rucksack again very much looking forward to the moment when I could dump it on the sofa at home and no longer need it. Walking out of the quiet low-lit stillness of the chapel I was reminded of Pilgrim and his progress. I suppose it is not surprising that I get asked about pilgrimage; different motivations for sure but parallels albeit centuries apart are undeniable, so here is the right place to share those pages from my notebook as written back at camp 10:

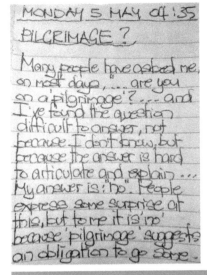

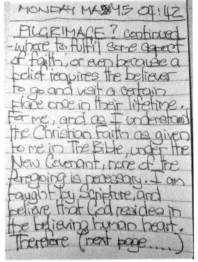

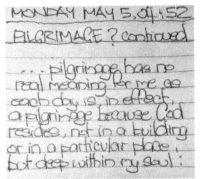

…all a bit of a long-winded, but there you have it. In summary, as many will agree, church is people not buildings, special as they undoubtedly are. They are all, whether large like the abbey or small like the chapel, places of worship, buildings where the church meets; but as we have seen during 2020 life goes on, even when buildings are shut, worship continues. I tend to prefer a hilltop, a forest, or a lonely beach but not always; I recognise my need of others.

With my arrival on Iona being a day earlier than expected, I spent the rest of the morning looking for accommodation for one night, so I could meet up with brother David (as in sibling not as in a religious order) and sister-in-law Janet on Wednesday morning as arranged. Unlike on Lindisfarne camping is permitted on Iona but once again I was seeking some home comforts. I had a note reminding me to enquire at the Iona hostel which I did, but the warden was away, in Mallorca of all places, presumably on holiday; so I never got to find out whether any accommodation was available. Having had an uneasy time at Camas, in truth, I was relieved.

Iona Hostel "Scotland's best eco-hostel"

Under perfect blue skies I enjoyed the walk to the north end of the island where the hostel is located so it was not a wasted journey. From the hostel I made my way to Iona's only official campsite to have a look how it had changed since the last time I saw it on my first visit to the island. To look you understand, I had absolutely no intention of camping, even if it was perfect camping weather. Having endured Mull's Jurassic coast I think I had overdosed; the draw of a B&B&B (this time the third B meaning bath not boat) was simply irresistible.

By the time I found a suitable B&B with a vacancy I felt I had walked another 10 miles. On Iona walking is the main way of getting around so it is easy to rack up the numbers. Unlike Lindisfarne visitors are not allowed to take their cars on to Iona. There are vehicles on the island but only ones as used by the residents and essential services.

Quoting welcometoiona.com:

"Iona is subject to a "Prohibition of Vehicles" Order that controls the type of vehicles allowed onto the Island. This Order was first introduced in 1978 to ensure the preservation of this popular island."

I saw a post van and a taxi. More information on their website.

Ruanaich

'Ruanaich' was my chosen B&B(&B) and was superb on account of location and everything else but particularly because the third B should actually have read J for Jacuzzi. Annabel the landlady offered it me as an option! After giving the matter no thought at all I 'opted in' and asked if I could indulge after an evening walk.

You would think after walking 300 miles I would be ready to put my feet up and watch telly for two weeks, but the reality is that stopping is harder than you might imagine because subconsciously a new rhythm has taken over. You cannot just hit the buffers; a gentle deceleration has to be the order of the day. With this in mind I set off walking again, this time unburdened, to Camas Cuil an t-Saimh (which translates 'The Bay at the Back of the Ocean') and eventually climbed up and on to the summit of Dùn I, the highest point on the island which is topped by an OS trig point at a modest 100 metres (328 feet) above sea level.

Getting there from the shore beyond the dunes at the northern end of the bay was way harder than I expected. Suddenly the hoped-for pleasant evening stroll turned into another game of snakes and ladders very similar to the one I had last played on the shore of Loch Lomond. Before indulging in more gaming I had a very important task to undertake; it was time to wet my boots by doing the obligatory salting ceremony, this time wetting them intentionally and in the sea as I had done on Lindisfarne two-and-a-half-weeks earlier.

Camas Cuil an t-Saimh ~ The Bay at the Back of the Ocean ~ seaweed and pebbles aspect

Back to the game: over a distance of about a mile I could see my objective all the time but getting to it got really frustrating. Instead of slowing down and chilling, I was scurrying up and down rocky knolls, getting already wet boots wetter still in the steep little valleys in between and generally wishing I hadn't

'Salting of the boots' ceremony

bothered, which on such an evening was properly ridiculous because the land and seascapes all around were stunning, and on this evening, deserted. Other than me it was sea, hills, and sky, plus sheep.

Iona was having the last laugh as I finally clawed my way up to the cairn. Once again I ate another sizeable chunk of humble pie having forgotten the golden rule of 'always respect the hill', whatever the size. The views all around were magnificent and extensive on all points of the compass from the

Paps of Jura in the south to the eye catching familiar shapes of the Treshnish Isles with low-lying Tiree and Coll to the north with the Rhum Cuillin just visible beyond, and Ben More on Mull in the east with the mainland shimmering in the distance; proving once again that even the smallest of hills can present challenges and then reward with the expansive views as magnificent as any you would care to mention.

Treshnish Isles ~ Bac Beag and Bac Mòr or Dutchman's Cap

Camas Cuil an t-Saimh ~ The Bay at the Back of the Ocean ~ grasses and sand aspect

Looking east from Dun-I towards Mull

Returning west directly down to the road near the abbey I retraced my steps back to ferry terminal and the nearby café and bar where celebratory fish n chips and a pint of Belhaven were duly consumed. With happy memories of a now seemingly distant adventure behind me I walked back to the B&B in the most beautiful lighting conditions of the entire journey. Dark clouds were brooding over Mull with the

The road to Ruanaich

occasional cluster breaking away west to quickly cross Iona drenching me with sun-soaked rain on their way. Then, almost as if I could grasp them, the sharp colours of a rainbow cut the sky. As I said at the beginning of this book I will let the pictures speak volumes I could never write. If we open our eyes He is there for all to see.

Back at the B&B&J it was time to submerge into a deep hot bath festooned with a dancing pile of foaming bubbles, most of which got out when I got in. Next time I use a jacuzzi I might exercise more caution in the bubble-bath and shower-gel departments. Heavenly.

I slept well. Tomorrow – the long journey home…

The Sound of Iona and a Promise

Sound of Iona

Admittedly, this page is a bit of a 'stocking filler' but in no way could I omit these delightful pictures of British Telecom's Iona HQ. I spotted this on my way back to the B&B… This was one of those rare 'double-take' moments when I could not quite believe what I was seeing. Note to BT: roof repairs needed. Call Cre8 on Macclesfield 503740!

BT Premises

Unauthorised access is trespass and is not permitted

Only for use by BT vehicles and other vehicles authorised to enter on business. All other vehicles are prohibited. BT will not accept liability for any loss, damage or injury, however caused, to unauthorised persons or vehicles.

Wednesday May 7, goodbye • Iona

Iona postal services

Departure day was bright and blue. In weather the likes of which I woke up to on this day, Iona is a vibrantly blue and green place, and after all the rain on Mull I was keen to get more of nature's elixir. I was keen to get out again. Romantic nonsense? Well maybe, but a budding writer must try. After a good breakfast at Ruanaich it was time to get going back towards the ferry, there were two passengers I was due to meet.

You would think in general that brothers should have good instincts for each other's movements, but not it seems on this Wednesday morning. Unknown to me David and Janet had arrived earlier than I was expecting; either that or somehow our paths must have crossed unawares which, within the confines of a small island village like Baile Mòr, is probably a trick I could not repeat. Either way we missed each other. We eventually met up just outside the grounds of the abbey. It was a real emotional high to be met by close family even if I did miss them on first go!

Those with sharp eyes will notice two things about the above picture: 1) that I clearly did not take it and 2) that I am wearing a lanyard. The latter because once again my expectations of a VIP welcome and wafting past the admissions cabin with a marching

Brothers grin ~ with lanyards resplendent ~ outside the abbey at St John's Cross

St Ronan's Bay

band in tow were unrealistic so I had to pay to get in like any other ordinary soul. I tried the "I've walked 300 miles from Lindisfarne" retort but to no avail; the attendant replied in other words: "they all say that!"

That's it, we're done! Those are my recollections of my 2014 walk across these British islands. During the afternoon David Janet and I crossed the Sound once more, this time together, back to Fionnphort; and caught a bus back to Craignure where we took rooms in the inn, drank, and ate our fill in the bar.

'Am fear a thèid a dh'I, thèid e trì uairean ann'.
A Gaelic saying meaning those who come to Iona will come, not once, but three times.
Goodbye Iona, until the next time.

Tomorrow Glasgow and home, but before I left Mull, I was already planning my next walk; the island traverse idea having got hold of me…

In 2016 on a wet morning in Lowestoft I set my sights west to Land's End and Cape Cornwall. Walking across Scotland from the north-east corner of England in 2014 confirmed my finding in 2005 that my island home was a lot bigger than I ever imagined. Turning my attention to the south of England and a journey from 'Far east to Far West' my perspective would change again as I paced across my island home. Step-by-step I was realising that I had only just started 'Sizing up Great Britain'. See you in Lowestoft?

Craignure

APPENDICES

1, 2, 3, 4 & 5

Gear, Clothing, Food, Drink, Maps, Data, Contact,
Day Section Index, Mileages.

Appendix 1 • Gear

Spot the brand!

As intimated in at least two places in this book, 'gear' for both camping and walking has sometimes resulted in one big fat disappointment, particularly in the boots and coats departments.

Getting equipped to go on a long walk, and especially if you want to travel as light as possible, can get very expensive. For example, these days you can buy tents so unbelievably feather-light that you can barely notice their addition to your rucksack but be prepared to pay; the lighter they get the more expensive they become! Another inconvenient truth is that for many people, myself included, for much of the year these costly items are in storage waiting for that next but all too rare adventure.

It was on a more recent walk that I saw a Tarptent Scarp 1 and it looked very good. The gentleman who was using it on a similar journey to my own was really pleased with it for being light, spacious, and easy to erect. One slight reservation is that I am not sure how I would regard the lack of privacy because with your light on after dusk these super-light models become somewhat 'veil-like'. More of a problem for two-persons I suspect! He paid handsomely for it – being imported direct from the USA that much was very clear. My chosen backpacking shelter is from much closer to home...

My trusty Terra Nova Equipment 'Laser Lite' tent (pictured below) is now, in 2021, in its 16th year and has been used on all of my backpacking walks and I have to say it has been consistently superb. The only slight gripe I have with it is its shape but much of that gripe is more to do with my age rather than any other factor. At either end headroom when horizontal is minimal to say the least, which is why I sometimes refer to it like being in a coffin (not that I have ever experienced that!) but in all other respects it works. It can sometimes be a struggle to withdraw the pole from the continuous sleeve when wet but again, a small criticism. More important than all of this the tent structure, on which ultimately it depends, and that has never failed. In my opinion Terra Nova really hold the gold-standard of UK lightweight tent manufacturing and will always be my first recommendation to anyone considering buying a lightweight tent. Brilliant, and a big thumbs up from me.

My Terra Nova 'Laserlite' tent undergoing Fabsil dowsing in my local Scout hall ahead of my 2018 walk

As for so-called 'tarps' I can absolutely assure you that I would never use one, certainly not anywhere north of Preston. How a tarp (short for tarpaulin) can be regarded as cool and more shall we say 'hip' with hordes of Culicoides impunctatus midges and other winged creatures bearing down on you is for others to answer. I will stick to my sealed in rip-stop nylon approach of an actual tent.

I commented at length about boots starting on page 128 so no need to repeat all that here, suffice to say that I still favour traditional leather construction over more recent fads for other materials with gawdy colours and seams galore. I have been on the conversion road once before with regard to walking poles so it might happen again, but I am yet to be convinced of the merits of anything other than leather. Likewise on the subject of **coats** I have also dealt with this at some length on page 165 so again, no need for repetition. These matters may well be regarded as better placed within these appendices, but I think they speak louder in the context of my walking recollections, so there they shall remain :)

Before I proceed to my list I want to talk about walking poles or sticks as they might be more traditionally described. Being a staunch fan of the late Alfred Wainwright I am very much influenced by his no-nonsense approach to such matters. Even in his mid to late seventies when filming an excellent series of programmes with Eric Robson (of BBC radio 4 Gardener's Question Time fame) I cannot recall Wainwright ever using a walking stick of any type. Knowing all of this and believing personally that we are fundamentally designed to walk on two legs not four, I used to view walking poles with derision, sometimes in private conversation with friends referring to large linear walking groups rather unkindly as 'caterpillars' because of all the legs and poles!

How wrong could I be. I could not help noticing, putting all my ill-informed opinions gripes and luddite attitudes aside, that I was in a minority of walkers by not using them. Everywhere I walked seemingly everyone had walking poles except for me. I had to investigate, there clearly was something in this walking pole malarkey.

My research took me to another great British company called Mountain King. I bought a pair of their 'Super Trekker' poles and have not looked back. I am a total convert. Using them, on every long distance walk since and including the one described in this book, has been part of the reason I have been able to walk so far. In those moments when the going was particularly tough as described in part two of this book, they were vital. They are also excellent for defending oneself against over-inquisitive herds of bovines as are encountered from time-to-time; and, with a Selfskie attached, can also help with photography! I would not be without them. For going downhill with a substantial weight on your back they are essential…

Mountain King both design *and* manufacture in the UK to super high standards and provide an excellent after-sales service. You can call them and get straight through to one of the people that actually make the products to order spare parts, which are always good value. In a world where designing 'planned obsolescence' into products has become all too common, Mountain King buck the trend and have won my custom and respect as a result. Highly recommended.

Finally picked out for special mention is my JetBoil cooker; or is it a stove? Having just checked the manufacturer's website I discover that it is a 'stove system'. I do not always enjoy the culinary delights that come out of it, but that is my problem! JetBoil has been my slightly angry friend since 2010 so now in its eleventh year of use. Another superb piece of kit; good design, well-built and reliable. I would like something a bit lighter but again the lighter you go the more money you part with. Gas supplies on route

JetBoil ~ the 'angry' one

can sometimes be a difficult to get hold of, so now I tend to use a larger canister than the one supplied that fits inside when packed away. This adds weight but provides adequate gas for up to a month on the trail and adds stability to the stove. With the small canister in use it is best to attach clip-on legs (as shown in the bottom left picture above) because when full it is very top heavy. Otherwise it's excellent.

My camera on this walk was loaned to me by my daughter Sarah because the camera on the mobile phone I had at the time was rubbish. If you look at the picture of the maps on page 151 you will see it used as a paper-weight!

It is tempting to get into a whole load of gear reviews here, but I need to keep this book affordable to produce, so on the next page you will find all my main pieces of kit listed in a table…

Item	Make/model	Website	My rating out of 10
Tent	Terra Nova Laser Lite 1	terra-nova.co.uk	9
Sleep mat	Thermarest ProLite regular	thermarest.com	9
Sleeping bag	Vango Venom 400 (3 season duck down)	vango.co.uk	8
Walking poles	Mountain King Super Trekker	mountainking.co.uk	9
GPS	Satmap Active 10	satmap.com	4
Stove	JetBoil	jetboil.com	8
Rucksack	Lightwave Wildtrek 70	lightwave.uk.com	9
Bivvy bag	Sol	surviveoutdoorslonger.com	-
Headtorch	Petzl (first generation)	petzl.com	6
Selfie stick	Selfskie (not used on this walk but mentioned above relating to walking poles)	selfskie.com	9
Compact Camera	Lumix digital 8x optical zoom 14Mpixel	panasonic.com	8

Appendix 2 ● Clothing

It has taken me years to finally settle on this most vexed of subjects. What you see in the picture to the left (apart from the few non-clothing items that have sneaked in) is my usual trekking wardrobe. Apart from the socks none of these items are expensive. The only clothes not shown in this pic are my PJs as they are way too personal to show; you will have to speculate on that one! Suffice to say as I mentioned at the end of part three, they are for me totally essential, especially when using a mix of accommodation in addition to camping.

Along with the Truswell Haulage cap my shirts have become a bit of a discussion point because in pictures I am rarely seen in anything else. It is a long-sleeved shirt made by Craghoppers and I have four of them, all identical apart from them being in different states of fading; a key feature of these shirts is the secret pocket which is always useful for tickets and the modest amount of cash I carry with me. At my supply points which are usually a week to ten days apart I always have replacements for all of the pictured items sent to me with any other bits and pieces of supplies I might need. All is parcelled up in a shoe box and sent ahead to an agreed address on route, be they post offices campsites or B&Bs etc., by Janine. Included in the box is always some sticky tape and a return label, already fixed under the address label, which I peel away after putting all my used stuff in the box. The system works well and has never let me down.

In my experience it is ironic but oh so predictable that my most expensive piece of kit, my raincoat, led as you will have read on page 165, to the most disappointment and discomfort. Mountain Equipment are a great local company based in Hyde near Stockport Cheshire not very far from where I live. They were very helpful and even replaced my coat for me ahead of this walk, as the first one I had was showing signs of waterproofing weakness in the few walks that I did leading up to this; but sadly the replacement was no better. Maybe I was just unlucky, I will perhaps try them again in the future if only to support local business.

Again, here is not the place for detailed reviews so once again I hope the table below will give a little insight…

Item	Manufacturer/style	Website/shop	My rating out of 10
Raincoat	Mountain Equipment Proshell	mountain-equipment.co.uk	6 & 10*
Over trousers	No idea but they were cheap!	millets.co.uk (probably)	7
Socks	1000 mile Fusion	1000mile.co.uk	9
Boots	Ex-military (German paras)	Stockport market	6
Gaiters	unbranded	millets.co.uk (probably)	7
Fleece	Epona Clothing Greenbelt 40 hoodie	epona-clothing.com	7
Shirt	Craghoppers Humbleton long sleeve	craghoppers.com	9
Trousers	Peter Storm 'Performance'**	peterstorm.com	7
Vest	Campri long sleeve baselayer	campri.com	9
PJs	Mind your own business	Definitely not!	10 ☺

* Only a 6 for the jacket but a big fat well-deserved 10 for the excellent customer service.

** I never wear shorts when hiking; partly for tick defence, partly so as not to scare the wildlife!

Appendix 3 • Food and Drink

Not a lot to say about this really other than I love indulging on my favourites. The great thing about walking for an extended period of time is that you can eat and drink (within reason) whatever you want. The liberation of being away from driving and not having to worry about it gives a feeling of freedom like no other, although you still must obey the law even when walking! When camping I eat very little actually at the tent. I might be found preparing porridge in the morning or maybe a Heinz Big Soup bought with pitta bread in a local shop for the evening if there was one at the end of a route day, but that is about as adventurous as I get. I definitely never use specialist 'trail foods' sold to the backpacker's market via specialist retailers online and on the high street. I much prefer to take my custom to local shops and buy ordinary stuff…

My favourite trail snacks are:

Mixed nuts and fruit (dried)

Cadburys Fruit and Nut Chocolate (when it isn't hot + one of my dad's favourites).

Real Lancashire Eccles Cakes (great for rotting your teeth).

Dried dates.

Mrs Crimble's Coconut Macaroons.

Sardines in brine (always carry a tin for emergency ration – last one I broke into was about 11 years old – it was perfect!).

Fresh fruit whenever I can get them.

Last but not least: Tunnock's Caramel Wafers made in Scotland!

I rarely have anything other than water with me and now use an ordinary plastic bottle put in one of the side-pockets of my rucksack carrying 500ml at the most and quite often I can go all day on that alone. On this walk I used a Platypus 'Hydration System' water bag with an 'irrigation' tube fed down into the purpose made sleeve in the back of my rucksack, but the water dispensed from it tasted really odd, so I have stopped using it. They are probably much improved these days, but I still feel a bit luddite about them much like I did about walking poles. Maybe I will see their merit eventually.

Off the trail and in the pub or café it is really easy to tell you what I have. Yes, you guessed it – fish n chips and a pint o' bitter please landlord! I sometimes get adventurous and try something different but not very often. Old habits die hard.

Appendix 4 • Maps, Data and Contact

Maps – do not get me started about maps. I am a self-confessed map-a-holic. I love maps! Regrettably, the harsh reality for me as a new author is that much as I would like to lavishly sprinkle the pages of this book with Ordnance Survey map extracts, I would have to pay dearly for the privilege and is therefore beyond the scope of this publication. However, being mindful that some readers may want to follow my route I make the following offer…

I am willing to send my route to you via email in GPX file format for import into commonly used GPS satellite navigation devices and online mapping services. In return, all I ask in exchange for the file, is a donation of a minimum of £10 to Cre8 in Macclesfield. Please contact them directly for payment details via email to hello@cre8macclesfield.org or by telephoning 01625 503740 ensuring that you give them your current, private (not business) email address.

Further information on the Cre8 website at cre8macclesfield.org

When I receive confirmation of your donation from Cre8, I will send the GPX files (split into three main sections because of intervening stretches of water) for the walk as featured in this book to you for your own personal use. Please note I cannot guarantee their accuracy in all locations.

Finally, I would love to hear from you! Your feedback and comments are welcome to paul@truswell.org. You can also find/follow me on Instagram @englishwildwalker.

Appendix 5 • Day Section Index and Mileages

Day	Page	From	To	Miles
1	19	Lindisfarne	Wooler	18
2	24	Wooler	Town Yetholm	13½
3	38	Town Yetholm	Eildon Hills	31
4	50	Eildon Hills	Traquair	19
5	68	Traquair	Romanno Bridge	18
6	76	Romanno Bridge	East Calder	16
7	86	East Calder	Polmont	17
8	94	Polmont	Kirkintilloch	19
9	104	Kirkintilloch	Drymen	20
10	112	Drymen	Cashel	11
11	118	Cashel	Inverarnan	19
12	134	Inverarnan	Dalmally	14
13	147	Dalmally	Portsonachan	9½
14	152	Portsonachan > boat > Taychreggan	Loch Nell	14½
15	159	Loch Nell	Oban (ferry to Craignure)	4½
15	164	Craignure	Glenbyre	16
16	172	Glenbyre	Camas (footway end)	20
17	182	Camas (footway end)	Fionnphort (ferry to Iona)	2½
17	188	Baile Mòr (Iona)	Iona Abbey	½

TOTAL 283

The beeline (straight line) distance between Lindisfarne and Iona is 184 miles.

By the time I add in diversions to various overnight stops and an allowance for going off course and having to retrace my steps on more than one occasion I reckon an actual total of 300 miles is about right.

This appendix 5 was very nearly forgotten. I added it on 31 July 2021 during my last weekend of final checks before publishing. It suddenly and somewhat belatedly dawned on me that this book's underlying theme of 'Sizing Up Great Britain' sort of demanded it! Never too late ☺